D0456314

Mountain Biking
the
Methow Valley

Help Us Keep This Guide Up to Date

Every effort has been made by the author and editors to make this guide as accurate and useful as possible. However, many things can change after a guide is published—trails are rerouted, regulations change, techniques evolve, facilities come under new management, etc.

We would love to hear from you concerning your experiences with this guide and how you feel it could be improved and kept up to date. While we may not be able to respond to all comments and suggestions, we'll take them to heart and we'll also make certain to share them with the author. Please send your comments and suggestions to the following address:

The Globe Pequot Press
Reader Response/Editorial Department
P.O. Box 480
Guilford, CT 06437

Or you may e-mail us at:

editorial@globe-pequot.com

Thanks for your input, and happy travels!

Mountain Biking
the
Methow Valley

Steve Barnett

FALCON®

Guilford, Connecticut
An imprint of The Globe Pequot Press

A FALCON GUIDE ®

Cover photo: Eric Sanford/Index Stock Imagery

Library of Congress Cataloging-in-Publication Data

Barnett, Steve, 1946–
    Mountain biking the Methow Valley / Steve Barnett.—1st ed.
        p. cm. (A Falcon guide)
    ISBN 1-56044-800-8
    1. All terrain cycling—Washington (State)—Methow Valley—Guidebooks. 2. Methow Valley (Wash.)—Guidebooks. I. Title. II. Series.
GV1045.5.W22 M483 2001
917.97'28—dc21

                                            2001033548

♻ Text pages printed on recycled paper.
Manufactured in the United States of America
First Edition/First Printing

Contents

The Trails

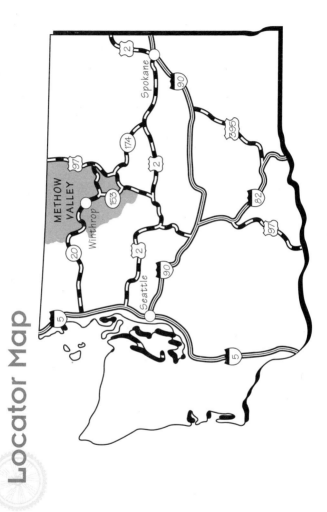

Locator Map

Legend

Interstate		Campground	
U.S. Highway		Building/Hut	
State or Other Principal Road		Pass/Saddle	
Forest Road		Peak/Elevation	4,507 ft.
Interstate Highway		Elevation	x 4,507 ft.
Paved Road		Gate	
Gravel Road		Parking Area	
Unimproved Road (doubletrack)		Overlook/Point of Interest	
Trail (singletrack)		Bridge	
Trailhead		Road Junction	
Trail Marker		Wilderness Boundary	
Waterway/Waterfall		Map Orientation	N
Lake/Reservoir		Scale	0 0.5 1
Meadow/Swamp			MILES

Overview Map

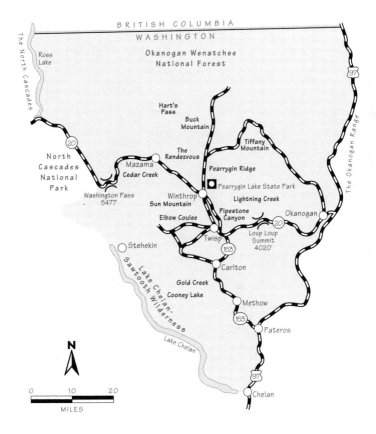

Introduction

Methow Valley Trails:
What to Expect

The Methow Valley extends from Mazama, deep in the wet, forested North Cascade Mountains, to Pateros, 60 miles to the southeast, which is part of the Columbia Basin desert. Its climate is completely unlike that of Puget Sound on the opposite side of the Cascade Crest. Even in Mazama there are many more sunny days and much less rain. Snow and cold in winter are reliable enough to sustain one of the nation's best cross-country ski areas with almost 120 miles of groomed ski track.

The peaks of the North Cascades rise almost 7,000 feet above the valley floor. They are rugged and alpine to the north and west and more gently rounded to the east. Though the valley borders the North Cascades National Park, the Pasayten Wilderness, and the Sawtooth-Chelan Wilderness, there is still so much legal trail to ride in the valley that it is basically infinite to the casual visitor. There is still a lot more trail than there are trail users.

Just as notable as the amount of trail is the variety of trail. There are rough high trails going through some of the finest alpine scenery you will ever see. There are smooth trails that your mother, and maybe your grandmother, would love. There are trails descending for 4,000 vertical feet of technically demanding singletrack, and several singletrack routes 30 miles or more long. Some trails will make you smile for hours; others will give you pleasure only in self-congratulation on your fortitude; and a few might make friends wonder about your sanity. We hope this guidebook will help direct you to the trails that fit your desires and ability, give you the information you need to get to the trailheads easily, and help you complete the rides safely without getting lost.

In general the farther east you go, the less precipitation there will be and the sooner snow cover will disappear in the spring. The earliest spring rides will be in the lowest and most eastern areas, such as Pipestone Canyon. Some rides even farther down valley open earlier, but they all include private land, and you'll have to make your own arrangements to ride them. The opposite strategy is needed in the hottest days of midsummer. High-altitude rides like those around Tiffany Mountain or above Cooney Lake will stay comfortably cool even when it's intolerably hot down on the valley floor.

There are three major networks of trail in the valley, as well as many individual trails. They are the Sawtooth Ridge network, the Beaver Meadow network, and the Sun Mountain network. The Sawtooth network is the highest in altitude, the most alpine, and the most beautiful, with many very long routes and lots of fast, moderate riding. The Beaver Meadow area is far to the east and less developed, with long trails, both moderate and very difficult. It is still in the process of development. Sun Mountain is the lowest and most developed of all the networks. It has well-marked easy to moderate trails, ranging in length in different combinations from short to long, with easy access and a long season. This is deservedly the most popular mountain-bike area in the Methow.

Many of the rides in this book go far into regions that are almost wilderness and are not often traveled. It's a lot better to ride out than to walk out. You want to avoid mechanical failures and to be able to repair most of those you can't avoid. Constant maintenance and checking of the chain, tires, wheels, brakes, shifters, derailleurs, etc. will go a long way toward preventing on-trail failures. Beyond that, carry a sell-stocked tool kit. It should include a pump, a spare tube and patch kit, a multitool with a chain tool, and duct tape and/or strapping tape. I include a spare cleat, a small Swiss army knife, and a pair of the smallest channel-lock pliers. Your fix-it kit will likely help repair someone else's bike as well as your own. It's larger than what you would carry for a two-hour race, but the situation is entirely different.

Some of the rides are long enough and go high enough that the weather can change radically while you are out. Many riders have set out for Starvation Mountain, for example, in summer conditions and then run into cold, rain, or even snow, with no quick way to get down and insufficient clothing to maintain body heat. Even fit riders can get in trouble this way. Prepare for the unexpected on these long rides. Carry a light, weather-resistant wind jacket and even a piece of insulated clothing, such as a stuffable, synthetic, water-resistant vest. These weigh very little and make a big difference if the weather makes a turn for the worse far from shelter.

For rides over two hours long, extra food is a necessity. Keep eating and you can keep going strong hour after hour. Given the often hot and dry summer climate in this area, carrying or finding enough water is essential as well for long rides. Mountain-bike country is often also horse, cattle, and hiker country. I usually carry a small bottle of water purification tablets (almost weightless) so I can take advantage of any water source along the way. You can also find filter-capped bottles, which you might find more palatable and easier to use.

Crashes happen. And they seem to happen about as often on easy, pay-little-attention parts of the trail as on gripping, obviously foolhardy, technically demanding sections. Carry a small first-aid kit consisting at least of bandages and tape. Alcohol wipes for cleaning wounds will help prevent infection.

One problem you will find when you set out to explore new rides is that no available map includes all of the roads and trails in the area. When the Forest Service discontinues a road or trail, it disappears from its maps and eventually from the maps of the USGS or Green Trails. On the ground it may still remain in good shape and be easily resuscitated for mountain-bike use (such as the Pearrygin Creek and Ridge Trails). We will try to provide adequate instructions and maps to help you navigate the trails described in this book.

District topo maps are available at $4.75 each from Methow Valley Ranger District, Okanogan Wenatchee National Forest, P.O. Box 188, Twisp, WA 98856; phone (509) 997–2131. They also have large district maps that cover the entire Methow Ranger District, as well as information about the condition of the roads and trails.

How to Use This Guide

Mountain Biking the Methow Valley describes 29 mountain-bike rides in their entirety.

Many of the featured rides are loops, beginning and ending at the same point but coming and going on different trails. The loop is by far the most popular type of ride, and we're lucky to have so many in the area.

Be forewarned, however: the difficulty of a loop may change dramatically depending on which direction you ride around the loop. If you are unfamiliar with the rides in this book, try them first as described here. The directions follow the path of least resistance and most fun (which does not necessarily mean easy). After you've been over the terrain, you can determine whether a given loop would be fun—or even feasible—in the reverse direction. Some trails are designated as one-way, so you don't have a choice.

Portions of some rides follow maintained dirt or even paved roads. A word about dirt roads: because the weather is so stable and dry much of the year, many dirt roads, though officially maintained, don't actually receive much attention. The surface may become loose because of accumulating sand and gravel, and washboard roads can be a pain.

Each ride description follows the same format:

Number: Rides are cross-referenced by number throughout this book. In many cases parts of rides or entire routes can be linked to other rides for longer rides or variations on a standard route. These opportunities are noted, followed by "see Ride(s) #."

Name: For the most part, I relied on official names of trails, roads, and natural features as shown on U.S. Geological Survey maps. In some cases deference was given to long-term local custom.

Location: Directions and approximate distances are from Winthrop and Twisp.

Distance: The length of the ride is given in miles, as a loop, or out and back.

Time: A conservative estimate of how long it takes to complete the ride: for example, 1 to 2 hours. The time listed is the actual riding time and does not include rest stops. Strong, skilled riders may be able to complete a given ride in less than the estimated time, while other riders may take considerably longer. Also bear in mind that severe weather, changes in trail conditions, or mechanical problems may prolong a ride.

Elevation gain: An elevation profile accompanies each ride description. Here the ups and downs of the route are graphed on a grid of elevation (in feet above sea level) on the left, and miles pedaled across the bottom. Route surface conditions (see map legend) and technical levels are shown on the graphs.

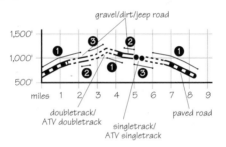

Note that these graphs are compressed (squeezed) to fit on the page. The actual slopes you will ride are not as steep as the lines drawn on the graphs (it just feels that way). Also, some extremely short dips and climbs are too small to show up on the graphs. All such abrupt changes in gradient are, however, mentioned in the mile-by-mile ride description.

Again, most of the rides in this book cover varied terrain, with an ever-changing degree of technical difficulty. Some trails are smooth with only occasional obstacles, and other trails are seemingly nothing but obstacles. The path of least resistance, or line, is where you find it. In general, most obstacles are more challenging if you encounter them while climbing than while descending. On the other hand, in heavy surf (e.g., boulder fields, tangles of downfall, cliffs) fear plays a larger role when riding downhill.

Understand that different riders have different strengths and weaknesses. Some folks can scramble over logs and boulders without a grunt, but they crash head over heels on every switchback turn. Some fly down the steepest slopes and others freeze. Some riders climb like the wind and others just blow . . . and walk.

The key to overcoming "technical difficulties" is practice: keep trying. Follow a rider who makes it look easy, and don't hesitate to ask for constructive criticism. Try shifting your weight (good riders move a lot, front to back, side to side, and up and down) and experimenting with balance and momentum. Find a smooth patch of lawn and practice riding as slowly as possible, even balancing in a "track stand" (described in the Glossary). This will give you more confidence—and more time to recover or bail out—the next time the trail rears up and bites.

Tread: The type of road or trail: paved road, maintained dirt road, doubletrack road, or singletrack.

Season: The best time of year to ride the trail.

Aerobic level: The level of physical effort required to complete the ride: easy, moderate, or strenuous.
  Easy: Flat or gently rolling terrain, with no steep or prolonged climbs.
  Moderate: Some hills; the climbs may be short and fairly steep, or long and gradual. There may be short hills that less-fit riders will want to walk.

Strenuous: Frequent or prolonged climbs steep enough to require riding in the lowest gear; requires a high level of aerobic fitness, power, and endurance (typically acquired through many hours of riding and proper training). Less-fit riders may need to walk.

Many rides are mostly easy and moderate but may have short strenuous sections. Other rides are mostly strenuous. Also be aware that flailing through a highly technical section can be exhausting, even on the flats. Good riding skills and a relaxed stance on the bike save energy.

Finally, any ride can be strenuous if you ride it hard and fast. Conversely, the pain of a lung-burning climb becomes easier to tolerate as your fitness level improves. Learn to pace yourself and remember to schedule easy rides and rest days into your calendar.

Technical difficulty: The level of bike-handling skills needed to complete the ride upright and in one piece. Technical difficulty is rated on a scale of 1 to 5, with 1 being the easiest and 5 the hardest.

Level 1: Smooth tread; road or doubletrack; no obstacles, ruts, or steep climbs. Requires basic bike-handling skills.

Level 2: Mostly smooth tread; wide, well-groomed singletrack or road/doubletrack with minor ruts, loose gravel, or sand.

Level 3: Irregular tread with some rough sections; slickrock, singletrack, or doubletrack with obvious route choices; some steep sections; occasional obstacles, including small rocks, roots, water bars, ruts, loose gravel or sand, sharp turns, or broad, open switchbacks.

Level 4: Rough tread with few smooth places; singletrack or rough doubletrack with limited route choices;

steep sections, some with obstacles; obstacles are numerous and varied, including rocks, roots, branches, ruts, sidehills, narrow tread, loose gravel or sand, and switchbacks.

Level 5: Continuously broken, rocky, root-infested, or trenched tread; singletrack or extremely rough doubletrack with few route choices; frequent, sudden, and severe changes in gradient; some slopes so steep that wheels lift off the ground; obstacles are nearly continuous and may include boulders, logs, water, large holes, deep ruts, ledges, piles of loose gravel, steep sidehills, encroaching trees, and tight switchbacks.

I've also added plus (+) and minus (-) symbols to cover gray areas between given levels of difficulty: a 4+ trail is harder than a 4 but easier than a 5-. A stretch of trail rated 5+ would be unridable by all but the most skilled riders.

Hazards: A list of dangers that may be encountered on a ride, including traffic, weather, trail obstacles and conditions, risky stream crossings, and obscure trails. Remember: Conditions may change at any time. Be prepared for storms, new fences, deadfall, missing trail signs, and mechanical failure. Fatigue, heat, cold, and/or dehydration may impair judgment. Always wear a helmet and other safety equipment. Ride in control at all times. If a section of trail seems too difficult for you, it's cooler to get off and walk your bike through the bad section than fly over your handlebars and break your collarbone.

Highlights: Special features or qualities that make a ride worthwhile (as if we needed an excuse!): scenery, fun singletrack, challenging climbs, or chances to see wildlife.

Land status: A list of managing agencies or landowners. Most of the rides in this book are on public land. These agencies have done a great job, along with the help of many volunteers, in creating a wonderful mountain-bike area.

Maps: A list of available maps. The Green Trails and U.S. Forest Service (USFS) maps were used for most of the rides. Not all routes are shown on official maps

Access: How to find the trailhead or the start of the ride, starting from a major street or highway in and around the Methow Valley. If you're lucky enough to live near one of the rides, you may be able to pedal to the start. For most riders it'll be necessary to drive to the trailhead or desirable to do a shuttle with two cars.

The ride: A mile-by-mile list of key points—landmarks, notable climbs and descents, wash/stream crossings, obstacles, hazards, major turns and junctions—along the ride. All distances were measured to the nearest tenth of a mile with a carefully calibrated cyclometer. As a result you will find a cyclometer to be very useful for following the descriptions. Terrain, riding technique, and even tire pressure can affect odometer readings, so treat all mileages as approximates.

One last reminder: The real world is changing all the time. The information presented here is as accurate and up-to-date as possible, but there are no guarantees out in the backcountry. You, alone, are responsible for your safety and for the choices you make on the trail. However, it's generally a good idea to bike with a partner—or to let somebody know where you're going and when you expect to return from an especially long or challenging ride.

If you do find an error or omission in this book, or a new and noteworthy change in a ride, I'd like to hear from you. Please write to Steve Barnett, c/o The Globe Pequot Press, P.O. Box 480, Guilford, CT 06437.

The Name Game

Mountain bikers often assign their own descriptive nick-names to trails. These nicknames may help to distinguish or describe certain parts of the overall ride, but only for those who know the nicknames. All too often the nick-names are meaningless—or misleading—to cyclists who haven't spun their pedals on the weekly group ride.

For the sake of clarity, I stuck to the official (or at least most widely accepted) names for the trails and roads described in this book. When a route is commonly known by more than one name, the other names are mentioned. If you know them by some other name, or if you come up with nicknames that peg the personalities of these rides, then by all means share them with your riding buddies.

Trail Manners

Respect for your surroundings is an essential element of mountain biking. We mountain bike partly to take in the sounds and sights of the wild wild woods, so let's treat our woods nicely. You've heard it a million times: don't litter, don't be excessively loud, and try not to run over centuries-old lichens. Joining a local mountain-biking organization and helping maintain trails is a fun way to preserve our trail network and generate good will toward mountain bikers.

Respectful behavior should extend to others you en-counter while riding. Yield to uphill riders. Yield to walk-ers. If there are horses, yield to them. It's better to respect other trail users and step aside for a minute than to have everyone get mad at you and see trail access for mountain bikes taken away. When a reckless rider roars down a hiking trail, causing the hiking family to haul up their three-year-olds by the shirt collars and dive to the side, we all lose. Like the finest Olympian profiled by tear-jerking up-close-and-personal TV coverage, be an ambassador for your sport!

IMBA Rules of the Trail

Thousands of miles of dirt trails have been closed to mountain bicyclists. The irresponsible riding habits of a few riders have been a factor. Do your part to maintain trail access by observing the following rules of the trail, formulated by the International Mountain Bicycling Association (IMBA). IMBA's mission is to promote environmentally sound and socially responsible mountain biking.

1. Ride on open trails only. Respect trail and road closures (ask if not sure), avoid possible trespass on private land, and obtain permits and authorization as required. Federal wilderness areas are closed to bicycles and all other mechanized and motorized equipment. The way you ride will influence trail management decisions and policies.

2. Leave no trace. Be sensitive to the dirt beneath you. Even on open (legal) trails, you should not ride under conditions in which you will leave evidence of your passing, such as on certain soils after a rain. Recognize different types of soils and trail construction; practice low-impact cycling. This also means staying on existing trails and not creating new ones. Be sure to pack out at least as much as you pack in. Some of the rides feature optional side hikes into wilderness areas. Be a low-impact hiker also.

3. Control your bicycle! Inattention for even a second can cause problems. Obey all bicycle speed regulations and recommendations.

4. Always yield trail. Make your approach known well in advance. A friendly greeting (or bell) is considerate and works well; don't startle others. Show your respect when passing by, slowing to a walking pace or even stopping. Anticipate other trail users at corners and blind spots.

5. Never spook animals. All animals are startled by an unannounced approach, a sudden movement, or a loud noise. This can be dangerous for you, others, and the animals. Give animals extra room and time to adjust to you. When passing horses use special care and follow directions from the horseback riders (dismount and ask if uncertain). Chasing cattle and disturbing wildlife is a serious offense. Leave gates as you found them, or as marked.

6. Plan ahead. Know your equipment, your ability, and the area in which you are riding—and prepare accordingly. Be self-sufficient at all times, keep your equipment in good repair, and carry necessary supplies for changes in weather or other conditions. A well-executed trip will provide satisfaction to you and not be a burden or offense to others. Always wear a helmet.

Keep trails open by setting a good example of environmentally sound and socially responsible off-road cycling.

Mazama and Highway 20 West

This area is wetter and steeper than the rest of the Methow drainage. There is more snow here. Trails close earlier and melt out later. Scenery and riding quality are both superb.

Early Winters Loop

Location: 4.5 miles west of Mazama on the valley bottom of Early Winters Creek.

Distance: 10.0 miles.

Time: 1–2 hours.

Elevation gain: 950 feet.

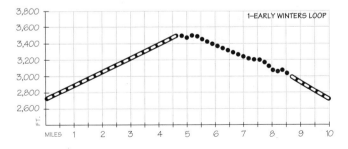

Tread: 3.9 miles on singletrack; 6.1 miles on pavement.

Season: Late spring through fall.

Aerobic level: Moderate.

Technical difficulty: 3; 4 on the 0.3-mile-long section of scree-covered trail.

Hazards: High-speed auto traffic on the North Cascades Highway (Washington 20). There is a short section of trail with steep sidehill exposure.

Highlights: Conveniently accessible, short singletrack near Mazama. Good views of high peaks near Silver Star Peak. Classic forest singletrack riding.

Land status: Okanogan Wenatchee National Forest, Methow Ranger District.

Maps: Green Trails, Washington Pass, WA–No. 50; USFS Winthrop W1/2 Ranger District map.

Access: From Mazama drive 4.5 miles up Washington 20 to the Klipchuck Campground turnoff. Pull off the road and park there. Alternatively, drive up Klipchuck Road and park in the Driveway Butte Trailhead parking lot, just before the campground itself.

The ride

0.0 Start riding to the west, up Washington 20 (the North Cascades Highway). Distances here are measured from parking by the Klipchuck Campground turnoff on WA 20.

4.7 The unmarked trailhead is just beyond the bridge over Early Winters Creek. Look for an opening in the woods to the right.

6.5 Start of scree-covered trail section.

· Early Winters Loop

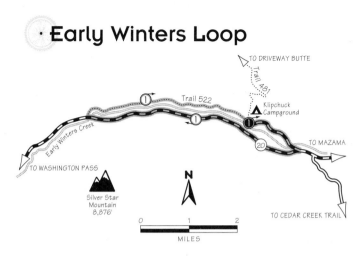

6.8 End of scree.

8.6 End of the trail in the middle of Klipchuck Campground. Head down the road to get back to Washington 20 and your vehicle.

10.0 End of the loop.

Driveway Butte Trail

Location: 6 miles west of Mazama on Washington 20.

Distance: 9.2 miles out and back.

Time: 4 hours.

Elevation gain: 3,100 feet.

Tread: 0.2 miles on gravel road: 9.0 miles on singletrack.

Season: Late spring to fall.

Aerobic difficulty: Strenuous.

Technical difficulty: 4.

Highlights: A tough climb, followed by an interesting ride through forest, leading to a spectacular valley-wide view.

Hazards: There is some steep sidehill exposure. The initial 2,000-vertical-foot climb is up a bare south-facing slope. Start early on hot days.

Land manager: Okanogan Wenatchee National Forest, Methow Ranger District.

Maps: Green Trails, Washington Pass, WA–No. 50; USFS Winthrop W1/2 Ranger District map.

Access: From Mazama drive west 4.5 miles on Washington 20 to the turnoff for Klipchuck Campground. Turn right and go 1.2 miles to the trailhead parking lot.

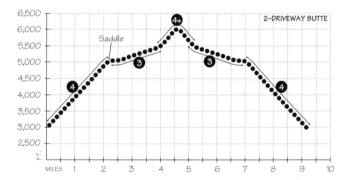

· Driveway Butte Trail

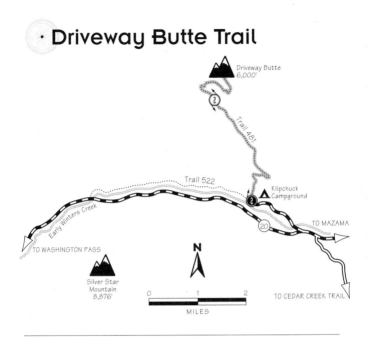

The ride

0.0   Cross the gate, follow the old road a short distance, and turn right on the marked trail.

1.5   Contemplate what will be a large drop-off over a root bundle for the return trip. Also note great views of Silver Star Mountain, the most beautiful peak in the area.

2.3   Reach the top of the climb up the bare, hot face of the mountain. Cross the saddle and immediately enter a cool forest environment.

4.1   The base of the summit ridge. The trail becomes indistinct here and if visible at all, goes straight up the steep slope. You will have to push or carry your bike up the trail.

4.6 The summit, site of an old, now destroyed lookout. There's a spectacular view of the entire upper Methow Valley. Return the way you came.

9.2 Back to the trailhead.

3

Cedar Creek Trail

Location: 5 miles west of Mazama near Washington 20.

Distance: 18.8 miles out and back.

Time: 5 hours.

Elevation gain: 3,460 feet.

Tread: All singletrack.

Season: Early summer through fall (at least to Cedar Creek forks).

Aerobic level: The first 7.4 miles, to the crossing of the Main Fork of Cedar Creek, ascend relatively gently, but the technical difficulties are great enough to make it at least moderate. The last 2 miles are steeper and rate as strenuous.

Technical difficulty: 4+. The first 2 miles are relatively easy and can be enjoyed by most riders. Beyond that, roots and rocks multiply to the point where good technical riding skills are necessary to enjoy the ride.

Hazards: There are a few sections with sidehill exposure. Unseen rocks like to grab pedals and stop wheels. This trail is popular with hikers and horseback riders, so be careful not to bomb too fast around blind corners.

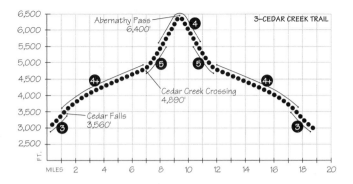

Highlights: The first 2 miles, up to Cedar Falls, make for easy, delightful riding for every rider. After that the rock gardens will challenge even adept riders. There are fine views on the upper part of the trail of the granite towers of Silver Star Mountain and Kangaroo Ridge.

Land status: Okanogan Wenatchee National Forest, Methow Ranger District.

Maps: Green Trails, Washington Pass, WA–No. 50; Green Trails, Mazama, WA–No. 51.

Access: From Mazama drive 4.2 miles west on Washington 20 to the sign for the Cedar Creek Trail. Turn left on the spur road and proceed 0.9 miles to the trailhead.

The ride

0.0   Start up Cedar Creek Trail.
1.7   Cedar Falls. The trail up to here and back is a good ride on its own and would be enjoyable for all riders. Beyond the falls the rock gardens multiply, and

· Cedar Creek Trail

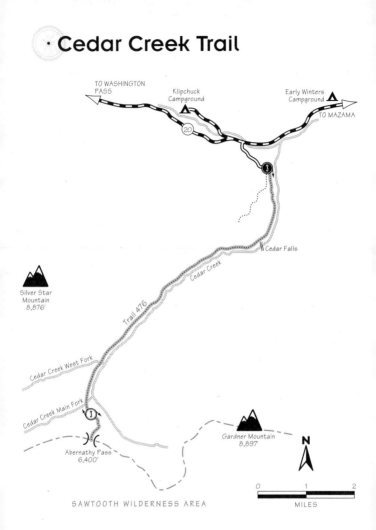

TO WASHINGTON
PASS

Klipchuck
Campground

Early Winters
Campground

TO MAZAMA

20

3

Cedar Falls

Silver Star
Mountain
8,876'

Cedar Creek

Trail 476

Cedar Creek West Fork

Cedar Creek Main Fork

3

Gardner Mountain
8,897'

N

Abernathy Pass
6,400'

SAWTOOTH WILDERNESS AREA

0   1   2
MILES

progress is more difficult than it should be for the modest overall grade.

6.6 Crossing of West Fork of Cedar Creek.

7.4 Crossing of Main Fork of Cedar Creek. Beyond this point the trail starts climbing steeply up to Abernathy Pass. The lower few hundred feet of this climb are very rough and washed out. Don't get discouraged. It gets better.

9.4 Abernathy Pass. Great views in both directions. Beyond here the trail enters the Sawtooth Wilderness Area and is forbidden to bikes. Turn around and enjoy the ride back.

18.8 Back at trailhead.

Virginia Ridge Loop

Location: 7 miles southeast of Mazama.

Distance: 6.5 miles.

Time: 1½ hours.

Elevation gain: 1,250 feet.

Tread: 2.8 miles on singletrack; 0.5 miles on doubletrack; 3.2 miles gravel road.

Season: Spring through fall.

Aerobic level: Moderate.

Technical difficulty: 3, punctuated by several sharp switchbacks.

23

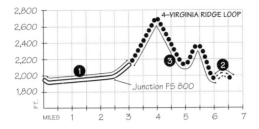

Hazards: There might be horse traffic on the singletrack.

Highlights: A delightful, smooth, singletrack ride through well-shaded forest. Easy access from Mazama. Low altitude means a long season.

Land status: Okanogan Wenatchee National Forest, Methow Ranger District.

Maps: Green Trails, Mazama, WA–No. 51.

Access: From the Mazama Store head back across the bridge to Washington 20 and turn left. At 5.2 miles you will reach the turnoff to Wolf Creek Road. From Winthrop go 8.8 miles west on Washington 20 to reach the same junction. Turn there and go 1.5 miles; cross a cattle guard. Just past that is a turnout to the right. Park there.

The ride

0.0 Continue riding south along Wolf Creek Road.

2.6 Turn right onto FS 800. The road climbs.

3.2 Just past the yellow STATE LAND sign on the left, look for a singletrack leaving the road to the left. The trail climbs 440 feet in several switchbacks.

4.0 The high point of the trail. A spur trail forks to the left and climbs 0.1 miles to a fine overlook of the Methow

Valley. The trail descends from here in several switchbacks.

4.4 Enter a large logging landing at the end of FS 800. Cross the road and go through a barbed-wire gate on the other side. The trail resumes.

5.0 Keep left here, staying on the singletrack. The doubletrack drops off to the right. The trail crosses a creek and then climbs.

5.4 The high point. The trail descends from here.

· Virginia Ridge Loop

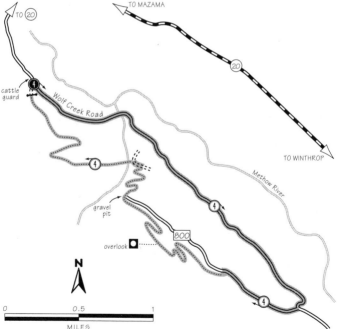

6.0 The trail ends in an old gravel pit. Continue straight across the opening and enter the doubletrack on the other side. It climbs a short distance. Stay on the doubletrack.

6.4 The doubletrack is now descending. Just before it runs into a **T** intersection, a singletrack branches off to the right. Take it and follow it down through the gate just above your parking spot. If you miss the singletrack, just turn right at the T and you'll end up in the same place.

6.5 End of the loop.

5

Methow River Trail

Location: 10 miles northwest of Mazama.

Distance: 16 miles out and back.

Time: 3 hours.

Elevation gain: 1,900 feet.

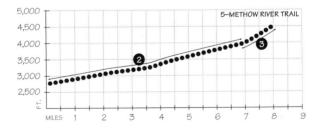

Tread: All singletrack.

Season: Late spring through fall.

Aerobic level: Moderate.

Technical difficulty: 2–3. Recently rebuilt to a very plush standard.

Hazards: Horse and foot traffic are to be expected, so keep an eye out. Going beyond the Pacific Crest Trail (PCT) junction is forbidden.

Highlights: It is hard to find a better trail for an easy ride with lovely scenery and some real wilderness. Low altitude allows a long season.

Land status: Okanogan Wenatchee National Forest, Methow Ranger District.

Maps: Green Trails, Washington Pass, WA–No. 50.

Access: From the Mazama Store go north along Lost River Road, past Lost River Bridge (7.0 miles), past the turnoff to Hart's Pass (9.5 miles), continuing until the road ends at the Methow River trailhead (9.8 miles).

The ride

0.0 From the trailhead cross Rattlesnake Creek and start pedaling southwest alongside the Methow River. The formerly very rough scree-surfaced trail has been filled in and is now almost highway smooth.

2.2 Cross the new bridge over Trout Creek.

3.7 The trail branch to the left leads to a nice campsite.

4.7 Break out of the trees and see more of the high country ahead.

6.8 The prow of Azurite Peak is dead ahead, dividing the canyon into two forks (Methow River and Brush Creek).

• Methow River Trail

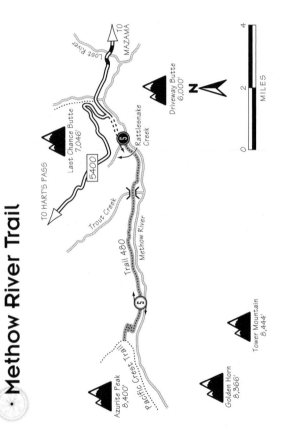

TO MAZAMA

Lost River

Last Chance Butte
7,046'

TO HART'S PASS

5400

Rattlesnake
Creek

Trout Creek

Driveway Butte
6,000'

N

Trail 480

Methow River

Pacific Crest Trail

Azurite Peak
8,400'

Golden Horn
8,366'

Tower Mountain
8,444'

0   2   4

MILES

7.1 First switchback.

8.0 Junction with the Pacific Crest Trail (PCT). Biking beyond this junction is forbidden. See glimpses of Tower Mountain and Golden Horn. Retrace your route back to the trailhead.

16.0 Back at the trailhead.

Rendezvous Loop

Location: 5 miles east of Mazama.

Distance: 9.6 miles.

Time: 1½ hours.

Elevation gain: 1,200 feet.

Tread: 2.9 miles on singletrack; 2.3 miles on doubletrack; 4.4 miles on pavement.

Season: Spring through fall.

Aerobic level: Moderate.

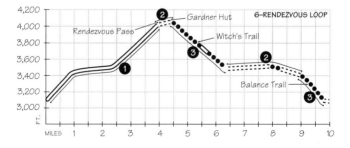

Technical difficulty: 3 on first 1.7 miles of Witch's Trail; 2 elsewhere.

Hazards: You might meet vehicles while climbing up Rendezvous Road. Watch out for cows on the trail. It's easy to lose Witch's Trail at its top; watch carefully for trail-marking ribbons.

Highlights: Easily accessible; close to Mazama; short enough for a quick morning or evening ride; provides a good chance to see wildlife; interesting riding.

Land status: Okanogan Wenatchee National Forest, Methow Ranger District.

Option: For a longer and harder ride, with less riding on gravel road, turn left up the Cassal Loop Trail at 0.9 miles, and follow that loop until it rejoins Rendezvous Road (FS 100). Then continue the route as described below.

Maps: Green Trails, Mazama, WA–No. 51.

Access: From the Mazama Store head southeast on Goat Creek Road, passing the Goat Creek turnoff and the entrance to Edelweiss. At 5.0 miles turn left on East Fawn Peak Road and climb 1,000 vertical feet (you can do this on your bike if you want a longer ride), past the Edelweiss junction, to the junction with Fawn Creek Road (FS 100). FS 100 continues as Rendezvous Road. Coming from Winthrop, turn right onto Goat Creek Road, go 0.4 miles, and turn right onto East Fawn Peak Road.

The ride

0.0   Start riding up the right branch of the road.
0.9   Cassal Hut trail junction. Keep going straight for the route described here or make an extension by going

Rendezvous Loop

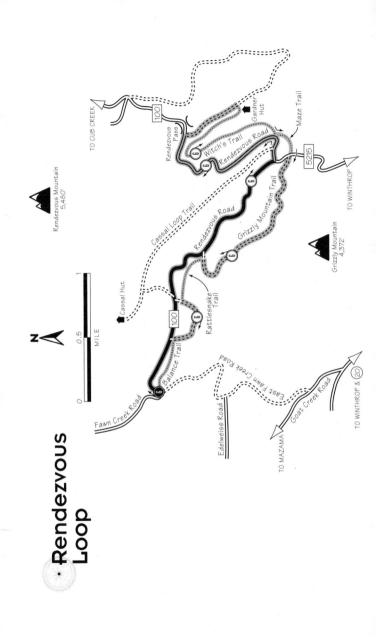

Rendezvous Mountain 5,480'

Grizzly Mountain 4,372'

TO CUB CREEK

100

Rendezvous Pass

Witch's Trail

Gardner Hut

Maze Trail

Rendezvous Road

5215

TO WINTHROP

Caesal Loop Trail

Caesal Hut

Rendezvous Road

Grizzly Mountain Trail

Rattlesnake Trail

100

Balance Trail

Fawn Creek Road

East Fawn Creek Road

Edelweiss Road

Goat Creek Road

TO MAZAMA

TO WINTHROP & 20

N

0   0.5   1

MILE

up the trail to the left and eventually looping back to Rendezvous Road.

2.4 Junction with FS 5215. Stay left.

3.9 Rendezvous Pass. Take the branch road to the right, which leads to Gardner Hut.

4.4 Gardner Hut. The start to Witch's Trail is a little hard to find. It's just above the hut and the trail parallels the road above. It is marked with occasional ribbons.

6.1 You are back momentarily on Rendezvous Road. Turn left, then left again, off the road and onto Maze Trail.

6.3 Junction with FS 5215. Cross it and follow Grizzly Mountain Trail.

7.9 The trail turns left off the doubletrack onto an easy-to-miss singletrack.

8.2 Junction with Rattlesnake Trail and FS 100. Keep left on Rattlesnake Trail.

8.3 Enter a large meadow. Stay left, following the edge of the meadow.

8.4 Go back into the woods on the doubletrack.

9.0 Junction with FS 100 and entrance to Balance Trail. Go left onto the trail, a nice piece of singletrack.

9.5 Balance empties back onto Rendezvous Road (FS 100). Turn left and ride the short distance back to your car.

9.6 End of the loop.

Canyon Creek Trail

While not actually in the Methow Valley, this trail is only 45 minutes from Mazama, closer than most Methow trails. Since it is an interesting trail and is on the route most people will take to get to the Methow Valley from Puget Sound, it is worth including.

Location: 45 miles west of Mazama on Washington 20, just east of Ross Lake. The other end, the abandoned mining settlement of Chancellor, is 27 miles northwest of Mazama via Lost River Road and Harts Pass Road (FS 700).

Distance: 9 miles one way or 18 miles out and back.

Time: 4 hours out and back.

Elevation gain: 3,800 feet out and back. Chancellor, the trail's end, is only 1,000 feet higher than the trailhead on Washington Highway 20, but there are an additional 1,400 feet of climbing due to hills and drops along the way.

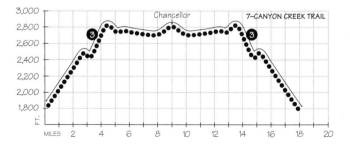

· Canyon Creek Trail

Tread: 18 miles on singletrack for the out and back route.

Season: Spring through fall.

Aerobic level: Moderate.

Technical difficulty: 3.

Hazards: There is serious exposure on a few of the sidehill trail segments overlooking the gorge of Canyon Creek. By all means get off the bike and walk these short sections if the exposure disturbs you.

Highlights: Low altitude. Scenic gorge. Mostly excellent tread. Good stop along the North Cascade Highway (Washington 20) between Puget Sound and the Methow Valley.

Land status: Mount Baker–Snoqualmie National Forest.

Maps: Green Trails, Mount Logan, WA–No. 49; USFS Winthrop W1/2 Ranger District map.

Access: The trailhead turnoff is at milepost 141.2 on Washington 20.

The ride

0.0 Start from the trailhead, crossing Granite Creek and then climbing up to the hillside along Canyon Creek.

2.0 Side trail to the left to Rowley's Chasm, a slot canyon dropping precipitously to Canyon Creek. Worth the short hike—but leave the bike behind.

4.1 Boulder Creek.

5.5 Mill Creek. Beyond the Mill Creek crossing, the trail becomes rough and overgrown. Persevere. It will improve, though not to the level it was before Mill Creek. It should be repaired in the next few years.

5.9 Mill Creek Trail junction. Mill Creek Trail is presently too overgrown to be followed.

7.4 Canyon Creek crossing.

9.0 The end of the trail at the abandoned mining camp of Chancellor.

18.0 Retrace your path back to the trailhead.

This is the highest legal bike area in the state. Any trip here will be among the most beautiful and exciting you can find anywhere.

Angel's Staircase Loop

Location: 25 miles south of Twisp, on Sawtooth Ridge between the Methow and Chelan Valleys.

Distance: 22.3 miles.

Time: 6 hours.

Elevation gain: 4,600 feet.

Tread: All singletrack.

Season: Summer and early fall.

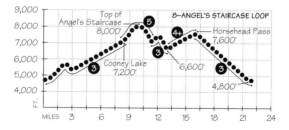

Aerobic level: Strenuous.

Technical difficulty: 4; 5 for a short distance.

Hazards: The trail is steep and rough at the top of Angel's Staircase. The weather can change dramatically during your ride on this very long, high-altitude route.

Highlights: Mountain scenery from the top of the world; larches that turn golden in the fall; beautiful Cooney Lake; varied, long trail reaching timberline, with long and exciting descents; a full day on your bike. One of the best rides anywhere.

Land status: Okanogan Wenatchee National Forest, Methow Ranger District.

Maps: Green Trails, Prince Creek, WA–No. 115; USFS Twisp Ranger District map.

Access: Head south from Twisp on Washington 20. At 2.4 miles continue straight on Washington 153 when Washington 20 turns left to Okanogan. Pass through the town of Carlton. Turn right onto Gold Creek Road (14.2 miles), right again on Gold Creek Road (15.3 miles), pass the South Fork and Foggy Dew junctions (19.8 miles), and follow signs to Crater Lake trailhead (27 miles).

The ride

- **0.0** Start up the trail from the 4,800-foot trailhead.
- **0.7** Take the left fork to Eagle Lake Trail (431).
- **2.5** Take the left fork onto Martin Creek Trail (429). This drops about 400 feet, then climbs again.
- **6.8** Junction with Martin Lakes Trail (429A). Keep left on Trail 429.
- **8.7** Cooney Lake (7,200 feet). Larch trees frame the lake amidst rich green meadows and rocky peaks. From

· Angel's Staircase Loop

Cooney Lake a steep side trail, No. 434, climbs 800 feet up to the ridgeline above. Take it.

9.5 Top out on a saddle overlooking Merchant Basin. Take the right fork here, which traverses the mountainside to reach the ridgeline to the west.

9.9 The top of Angel's Staircase. There are fantastic views of green meadows and high peaks. The way down is steep and rocky. You might have to walk the top section.

11.3 Junction with trail 1259. Turn right.

13.5 Junction with trail 431. Turn right and climb to Boiling Lake.

14.5 Boiling Lake. The trail climbs steeply from here. This formerly unridable climb has recently been improved.

15.5 Horsehead Pass.

16.5 Junction with Upper Eagle Lake Trail. Keep straight on trail 431.

19.8 Junction with trail 429. Keep left. From here you are retracing your path to the trailhead.

22.3 Crater Lake trailhead and car.

Foggy Dew—Merchant Basin and Cooney Lake

Location: In the high peaks adjacent to the Sawtooth-Chelan Wilderness Area, 25 miles southwest of Twisp.

Distance: 16.0 miles.

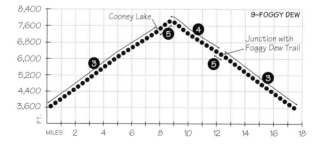

Time: 5 hours.

Elevation gain: 4,400 feet; 3,800 feet if you go just to Cooney Lake and back.

Tread: All singletrack.

Season: Summer and fall.

Aerobic level: Strenuous.

Technical difficulty: 5 on the Merchant Basin Loop; 3 if you just do Cooney Lake out and back.

Hazards: This long, high-elevation route is subject to quickly changing mountain weather. Carry extra weather-protective clothing, extra food, and a water filter or iodine tablets. There is a difficult, exposed section of trail below Merchant Basin.

Highlights: This ride has wonderful scenery and an outstanding descent down Foggy Dew Creek. That descent is fast, stupendously long, and easy, without being buffed completely smooth. In the fall Cooney Lake is surrounded by golden larch trees. Merchant Basin is as high as you can get on a bike in the North Cascades. If the high altitude and technical difficulties above the lake don't entice you or your group, the ride to the lake and back is outstanding in its own right.

Land status: Okanogan Wenatchee National Forest; Methow Ranger District.

Maps: Green Trails, Prince Creek, WA–No. 115.

Access: Head south from Twisp on Washington 20. At 2.4 miles continue straight on Washington 153 when Washington 20 turns left to Okanogan. Pass through the town of Carlton. Turn right onto Gold Creek Road (14.2 miles), right again on Gold Creek Road (15.3 miles), and follow the signs for the Foggy Dew trailhead (23.4 miles).

Foggy Dew

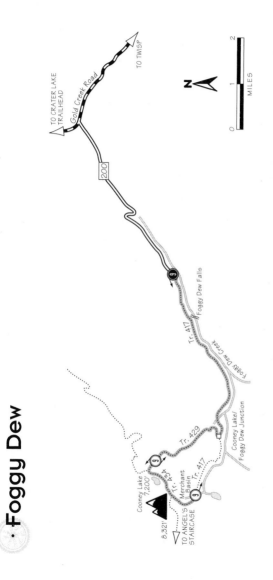

TO CRATER LAKE TRAILHEAD

Gold Creek Road

TO TWISP

200

N

0   1   2
MILES

Foggy Dew Falls

Tr. 417

Foggy Dew Creek

Cooney Lake/
Foggy Dew Junction

Tr. 429

Cooney Lake
7,200'

Tr. 429

8,321'

Merchant
Basin

Tr. 417

TO ANGEL'S
STAIRCASE

The ride

0.0   Head west up trail 417.

2.8   Foggy Dew Falls.

5.0   Junction with trail 429. Go right. The left-hand trail comes down from Merchant Basin.

7.7   Cooney Lake junction. Turn left to get to the lake. Turning right will take you to the Crater Creek trailhead—another great ride.

7.9   Cooney Lake. This beautiful lake, 7,200 feet high, is surrounded by high peaks and alpine larches. It is the turnaround point if you don't want to go on to Merchant Basin. The return trip is a wonderful, moderate downhill ride. The going gets much more difficult above the lake. Find the unmarked trail climbing around the south side of the lake. This gets very steep and rough as it approaches the pass 800 feet higher. Expect to walk.

8.7   The top—the 8,000-foot divide between Cooney Lake and Merchant Basin. A branch runs off to the right to the top of Angel's Staircase, part of another sensational trail loop. Heading straight, down into Merchant Basin, the top section is loose but ridable. The main difficulty is clearing the unusual stone water bars.

10.5 The trail becomes steep, loose, and exposed as it switchbacks down from 6,500 feet to 6,300 feet.

11.0 Junction with Cooney Lake–Foggy Dew Trail. From here the trail is fantastic, much easier and faster than above.

16.0 Back at Foggy Dew trailhead.

Beaver Creek Area

The trails here are among the most popular in the Methow Valley. The area is relatively dry and melts out early in the spring.

Pipestone Canyon
Easy Loop

Location: 8 miles east of Twisp in the foothills of the Okanogan Range.

Distance: 11.9 miles.

Time: 2½ hours.

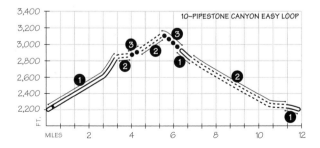

Elevation gain: 1,450 feet.

Tread: 2.7 miles on singletrack; 4.2 miles on doubletrack; 5.0 miles on gravel road.

Season: Spring through fall.

Aerobic level: Moderate.

Technical difficulty: 3. There are some rocks on the doubletrack and there is a short, steep, and loose descent on the singletrack.

Hazards: Rattlesnakes are common in Pipestone Canyon when it's hot.

Highlights: Low elevation and a dry location make this ride a good choice very early or very late in the season. It's a fun and scenic downhill trip through the canyon.

Land status: Washington State Department of Fish and Wildlife.

Maps: Green Trails, Twisp, WA–No. 84.

Access: From Twisp drive south on Washington 20. At 2.5 miles turn left, toward Okanogan (you are still on Washington 20). At 5.6 miles turn left onto Beaver Creek Road. Follow that past the junction with Balky Hill Road to a wide area off the road at pavement's end, just past the cattle guard (8.7 miles).

The ride

0.0 Begin pedaling north up Beaver Creek Road.
2.2 Cross a bridge over Beaver Creek. Immediately afterwards turn left onto Lester Road.
2.7 Go left onto the primitive doubletrack.
3.5 The doubletrack ends, but keep right. A trail contours down the hillside, crosses the flat, and then

Pipestone Canyon Easy Loop

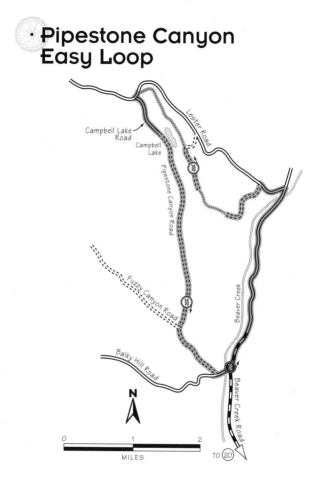

Campbell Lake Road

Campbell Lake

Lester Road

Pipestone Canyon Road

Fuzzy Canyon Road

Beaver Creek

Balky Hill Road

Beaver Creek Road

N

0   1   2
MILES

TO 20

starts up the little valley ahead. It becomes double-track again.

4.9 The doubletrack leaves the little valley and turns right. A singletrack runs straight ahead. Take it.

6.2 The trail meets Lester Road. Turn left.

6.3 Junction. Turn left onto Campbell Lake Road.

7.2 Campbell Lake.

7.5 Entrance to Pipestone Canyon. Leave the gates as you find them. After exiting the canyon keep cruising down the valley through open fields.

10.0 Junction with Fuzzy Canyon Road. Continue straight down the valley to its meeting with Balky Hill Road.

10.8 Balky Hill Road. Turn left

11.3 Beaver Creek Road. Turn left.

11.9 End of the loop.

Pipestone Hard Loop

Location: 11 miles east of Twisp in the foothills of the Okanogan Range.

Distance: 10.8 miles.

Time: 2–3 hours.

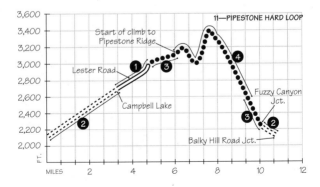

Elevation gain: 1,770 feet.

Tread: 5.4 miles on singletrack; 4.0 miles on doubletrack; 1.4 miles on gravel.

Season: Spring through fall.

Aerobic level: Strenuous. There are several very steep climbs on sketchy trail.

Technical difficulty: 4. The descent off of the ridgetop is steep and rocky.

Hazards: Gawk too far and you might fall off the edge of Pipestone Canyon. Steep, rocky trail descent demands caution. There may be rattlesnakes on the road through the canyon.

Highlights: Scenic edge of Pipestone Canyon demands gawking. Great views of the North Cascades as well. The snow disappears earlier than on any other technical route in the area, and the riding often remains good late into the fall. Not least, the riding is excellent—technically challenging and exhilarating.

Land status: Washington State Department of Fish and Wildlife.

Option: To be able to bike to the ride from Winthrop or to get a longer ride, with about 500 feet more vertical, start riding from the junction of Bear Creek Road and Campbell Lake Road as in Ride 21.

Maps: Green Trails, Twisp, WA–No. 84.

Access: From Twisp drive south on Washington 20. At 2.5 miles turn left, following Washington 20. At 5.6 miles turn left onto Beaver Creek Road. Turn left at the junction with Balky Hill Rd at 8.1 miles. Go 0.5 miles farther and park at the corner where the road turns left and climbs. On the right a dirt road leads to Pipestone Canyon.

· Pipestone Hard Loop

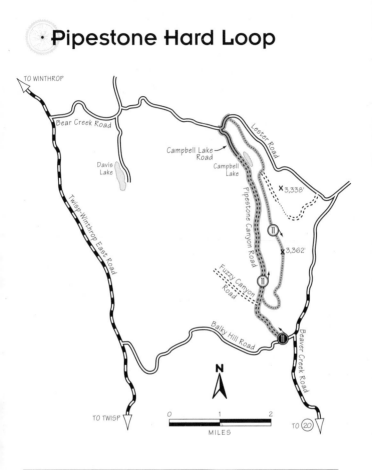

The ride

0.0 Start north up Pipestone Canyon Road.

0.7 Junction with Fuzzy Canyon Road. Keep right. Pedal up Pipestone Canyon Road through Pipestone Canyon.

3.3	The end of the canyon. Campbell Lake is just ahead.
4.6	Junction with Lester Road. Turn right.
4.7	Take the singletrack that starts out on the right side of the road.
5.9	The trail forks. Go right.
6.0	There is another trail junction, but its right branch, the one you want, is faint. It goes up the end of the ridgeline, while the main branch goes down into the valley below the ridge. Follow the trail up the ridge and along its left side, going by the tops of the Pipestone Canyon hoodoos, the freestanding stone pillars created by erosion.
6.9	The trail drops to a saddle. It continues on the far right side of the open slope.
7.5	The high point of the ridge. The trail continues along the ridge crest. Then it becomes steep, rocky, and technically difficult as it descends the ridge.
10.1	Junction with Pipestone Canyon Road. Turn left, back to the starting point.
10.8	Junction with Balky Hill Road and parking spot.

Bear Mountain Figure 8

Location: 13 miles east of Twisp in the Beaver Creek drainage.

Distance: 15 miles.

Time: 3 hours.

Elevation gain: 2,400 feet.

Tread: 6.1 miles on singletrack; 8.9 miles on gravel road.

Season: Spring through fall.

Aerobic level: Moderate.

Technical difficulty: 4 on Middle Fork Trail; 3 on Bear Mountain Trail.

Hazards: The Middle Fork Beaver Creek Trail has steep and loose sections as well as areas with steep sidehill exposure.

Highlights: This route ties two excellent singletrack downhills together with climbs up good gravel roads. Because of the low altitude and easterly location, the trail opens relatively early in the spring.

Land status: Okanogan Wenatchee National Forest, Methow Ranger District.

Maps: Green Trails, Loup Loup, WA–No. 85; USFS Twisp Ranger District map.

Access: From Twisp head south on Washington 20, turning left at 2.5 miles toward Loup Loup summit. At 5.4 miles turn left again at the signed intersection with Beaver Creek Road and follow that to the junction with the South Summit Road (FS 4225) at 11.4 miles. Keep right on South Summit Road. Park at the junction with the Middle Fork of Beaver Creek at 13.0 miles.

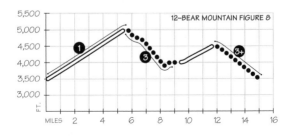

· Bear Mountain Figure 8

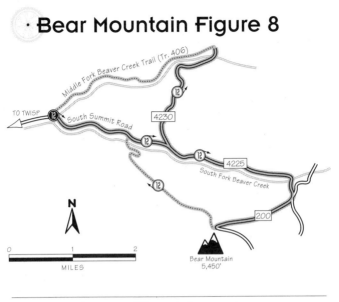

MILES

Bear Mountain
5,450'

The ride

0.0 Start riding east up South Summit Road (FS 4225).

2.3 Junction with FS 4230. Keep going straight.

4.0 Turn right at the junction onto FS 200. This is just before FS 4225 turns to pavement. There is a gate at the start of FS 200.

5.6 Reach a hairpin heading uphill. Look downhill from the hairpin and you will see the Bear Mountain trailhead. This trail is new, built for mountain biking, and only moderately difficult, with a few technical challenges scattered along its length.

5.9 A wet, swampy section. Logs to the right provide a drier crossing. The trail then follows the ridge.

7.6 The trail crosses a logging spur road. Then it drops down in a series of switchbacks to South Fork Beaver Creek.

8.4 The trail crosses South Fork Beaver Creek, then climbs up to the road. You may have to take off your shoes and socks and wade across when the creek is high in the spring or after a heavy rain.

8.5 Junction with South Summit Road. Turn right. Start climbing up the road again. This is the crossing part of the figure 8.

9.5 Turn left at the junction, onto FS 4230.

11.6 Cross Middle Fork Beaver Creek. Right after the crossing there is a spur to the left. Follow it down, keeping on the right side of the clearing.

11.8 Middle Fork Trail starts from the clearing. It's an old one, recently rehabilitated. This trail is rougher and more challenging than Bear Mountain Trail, though its most difficult, interesting, and death-defying technical section was eliminated in the rehabilitation. See if you can still find it.

15.0 Junction with South Summit Road and end of the loop.

Lightning Creek Trail

Location: 11.5 miles southeast of Twisp in the Beaver Creek drainage.

Distance: 15.3-mile loop.

Time: 3–4 hours.

Elevation gain: 2,600 feet.

Tread: 6.4 miles on singletrack; 8.9 miles on gravel road.

Season: Late spring through fall.

Aerobic level: Moderate, except for a very short section of steep singletrack on the ascent.

Technical difficulty: 3+. The trail is loose and sandy for a short distance midway.

Hazards: Some sidehill exposure. Stream crossings might be high in the spring.

Highlights: Climb on easy road; descend on moderate, long singletrack. The trail melts out early and is on the dry eastern side of the Methow Valley.

Land status: Okanogan Wenatchee National Forest, Methow Ranger District.

Maps: Green Trails, Twisp, WA–No. 84; Green Trails, Loup Loup, WA–No. 85; USFS Twisp Ranger District map.

Access: Go south out of Twisp on Washington 20, turning left toward Loup Loup Pass at 2.5 miles from the center of Twisp. At 5.5 miles turn left onto Beaver Creek Road. At 11.5 miles you will reach the junction of Volstead Creek and South Fork Beaver Creek Roads. Park there.

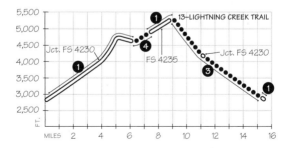

The ride

0.0 Start riding east up South Fork Beaver Creek Road (FS 4225).

1.8 Junction with Middle Fork Beaver Creek Trail (FS 406). Continue straight on FR 4225.

3.1 Junction with Bear Mountain Trail (FS 442). Continue straight on FR 4225.

4.1 Junction with FS 4230. Turn left.

5.1 High point. Descend slightly to Middle Fork Beaver Creek.

6.3 Cross Middle Fork Beaver Creek. Turn right onto trail FS 406. Climb 200 feet to the road above, FS 4235, and turn left onto it.

8.9 Cross Lightning Creek.

9.1 Lightning Creek trailhead is on your left. Start down the trail.

10.9 Junction with FS 4230. Turn right.

11.0 Lower Lightning Creek trailhead. Turn left, resuming the descent on FS 425. The first 0.25 mile or so is sandy and loose.

13.5 Cross the creek. There is a handy log and stepping stones if it's too high to ride across.

13.6 Cross the creek again, then almost immediately pass the Blue Buck Trail junction. Continue on lower Lightning Creek trail.

13.7 Cross the bridge over Beaver Creek.

14.9 The trail exits into a primitive campground.

15.0 Junction with FS 200. Turn left.

15.4 Your car and the end of the loop.

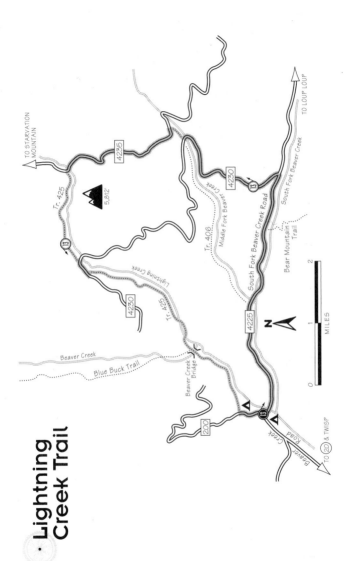

Lightning Creek Trail

Starvation Mountain Loop

Location: 11 miles east of Twisp on the ridge between the Methow and Okanogan Valleys.

Distance: 25.7 miles.

Time: 6 hours.

Elevation gain: 4,280 feet.

Tread: 21.1 miles on singletrack; 4.6 miles on gravel road.

Season: Late spring to early fall.

Aerobic level: Strenuous.

Technical difficulty: 3.

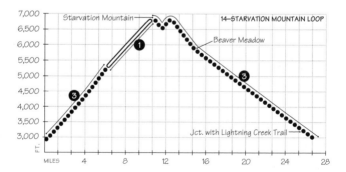

Hazards: Severe weather can develop rapidly at the high altitudes reached by this long loop. Be prepared for cold and/or wet conditions even if things look perfect when you start.

Highlights: High altitude cools the ride on a hot day. There is an exceptionally long, but moderate, downhill. Beaver Meadow is a beautiful spot to visit.

Land status: Okanogan Wenatchee National Forest, Methow Ranger District.

Maps: Green Trails, Doe Mountain, WA–No. 52; Green Trails, Tiffany Mountain, WA–No. 53; Green Trails, Twisp, WA–No. 84; Green Trails, Loup Loup, WA–No. 85; USFS Twisp Ranger District map.

Access: Go south out of Twisp on Highway 20, turning left toward Loup Loup Pass 2.5 miles from the center of Twisp. At 5.6 miles turn left onto Beaver Creek Road. At 11.5 miles you will reach the junction of Volstead Creek and South Fork Beaver Creek Roads. Go about 0.33 mile beyond this junction. The Lightning Creek Trailhead is in the camping area to the right.

The ride

0.0 Start up Lightning Creek Trail.
1.2 Cross Beaver Creek. The junction with Blue Buck Trail is just beyond the bridge. Keep right on Lightning Creek Trail.
1.4 Ford Lightning Creek.
1.6 Ford Lightning Creek again. Continue up the trail.
4.0 Junction with FS 4230. Dogleg to the right a few hundred yards and pick up the trail again on the other side of the road.

· Starvation Mountain Loop

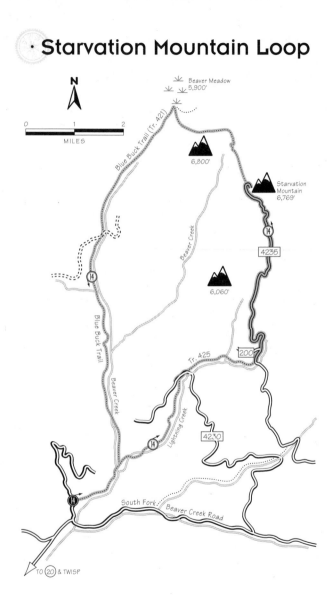

N

0   1   2
MILES

Beaver Meadow
5,900'

Blue Buck Trail (Tr. 421)

6,800'

Starvation
Mountain
6,769'

14

4235

Beaver Creek

6,060'

Blue Buck Trail

Beaver Creek

14

Tr. 425

200

4230

Lightning Creek

14

South Fork   Beaver Creek Road

14

TO 20 & TWISP

6.1   Junction with FS 4235. Don't take the sharp left turn at this junction onto FS 200, which goes nowhere. Follow FS 4235 left, up to its end at Starvation Mountain summit.

10.6   The summit. Backtrack a little to find the primitive, very rough fire road dropping off the summit to the NNW. An alternative is a singletrack, closer to the summit, which drops down to the same saddle NNW of the summit and joins the fire road. The fire road then climbs up to a second summit and drops down its other side.

14.6   Junction with Blue Buck Trail No. 421. Continuing straight will take you to Beaver Meadow, which is off of the loop but a beautiful spot. Blue Buck Trail heads to the left. The top third is a great section of singletrack.

17.6   The trail dumps onto a rough logging spur. Keep an eye peeled to the right for the resumption of the trail above the spur. Cross a road and continue on the trail in the woods on the other side. The trail eventually breaks out onto a very long section of moderate sidehill riding.

24.0   Switchback.

24.2   Cross Beaver Creek.

24.5   Junction with Lightning Creek Trail, then cross Beaver Creek again.

25.7   End of loop.

Northeast of Winthrop

This area has very long and technically interesting rides. High altitude on some trails allows cool riding on hot summer days.

North Twentymile Trail

Location: 19 miles north of Winthrop on the east side of the Chewuch River.

Distance: 12 miles round-trip.

Time: 6 hours.

Elevation gain: 4,400 feet (5,000 from Chewuch River Road).

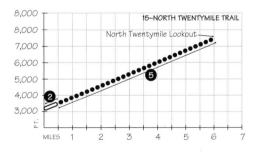

· North Twentymile Trail

Tread: 11 miles on singletrack; 1 mile on doubletrack.

Season: Late spring through fall.

Aerobic level: Strenuous.

Technical difficulty: 5.

Hazards: High mountain environment subject to sudden severe weather. Serious rock gardens and other technical difficulties on the way down.

Highlights: This is the longest, most intense, most continuously technically demanding, and most satisfying of all the local downhill rides. The view at the top is spectacular. Traversing North Twentymile Ridge from the top is a fine ride on its own.

Land status: Okanogan Wenatchee National Forest, Methow Ranger District.

Maps: Green Trails, Doe Mountain - No. 52; Green Trails, Coleman Peak - No. 20; USFS Tonasket W1/2 Winthrop E1/2 District map.

Access: Follow Washington 20 north out of Winthrop until, just before the baseball field, West Chewuch Road forks off to the right. In about 17 miles you'll reach Camp 4 Campground. Just beyond that is a bridge to the right, crossing the Chewuch River. Cross it, and head south back down river a short distance until you reach FS 700. Turn left and go 1.5 miles up FS 700. There is a parking area and a sign for the North Twentymile Trailhead. If you're willing to do the extra vertical, it's fun to ride all the way down to the Chewuch Road junction.

The ride

- **0.0**   Start up the trail. The first few hundred feet of climbing are on a rough (now closed to vehicles) doubletrack.
- **0.5**   Start of singletrack. The first 1,000 vertical feet are somewhat loose and sandy.
- **6.0**   North Twentymile Lookout. From here you can go out along North Twentymile Ridge, following the trail as far as seems interesting, and then return for the descent. North Twentymile Ridge eventually leads to Smarty Creek Trail and the road to Loomis. This can be used for a loop but it is very long, spends a lot of time on uninteresting road, and was consid-

erably damaged by both the devastating 1994 Thunder Mountain Fire and the efforts to fight it. Out and back is my strong preference.

12.0 Trailhead.

Pearrygin Creek Trail

Location: 6 miles northeast of Winthrop, above Pearrygin Lake State Park.

Distance: 10.4-mile loop.

Time: 3 hours.

Elevation gain: 1,850 feet.

Tread: 4.5 miles on singletrack; 5.9 miles on gravel road.

Season: Spring through fall.

Aerobic level: Strenuous.

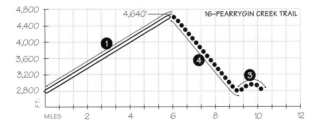

Technical difficulty: Some of the ride is 4+, where there are loose, steep descents and sharp **V** turns on sidehills.

Hazards: There are long stretches of steep sidehill where a fall could lead to an unpleasant slide. Many trail sections become loose in the dry season. You might run into cows on the trail.

Highlights: This is an interesting, difficult trail, close to Winthrop. It is low enough to melt out early in the spring. It connects to the Pearrygin Ridge Trail (Ride 17) to form part of a long loop through Beaver Meadow, down Blue Buck Trail, and back to Winthrop.

Options: Connect this with the Pearrygin Ridge Trail (Ride 17) up to Pearrygin Peak for a long out-and-back trip (18.3 miles and 4,000 vertical feet).

Land status: Okanogan Wenatchee National Forest, Methow Ranger District.

Maps: Green Trails, Doe Mountain, WA–No. 52; USFS Tonasket W1/2 Winthrop E1/2 Ranger District map.

Access: From Winthrop, drive north on East Chewuch Road. At 1.5 miles take the turnoff right to Pearrygin Lake. At 3.4 miles continue past the next turnoff to the lake. The pavement ends and the road climbs a little. At the junction turn left toward Sullivan Pond on FS 100 and continue. At 5.8 miles, park on the east side of the pond.

The ride

0.0 Ride up FS 100, pass FS 200, and continue straight on FS 300 (signed PEARRYGIN RIDGE).

5.9 Reach a right-hand corner with a stock watering tank on your left. On the right look for a cairn and

· Pearrygin Creek Trail

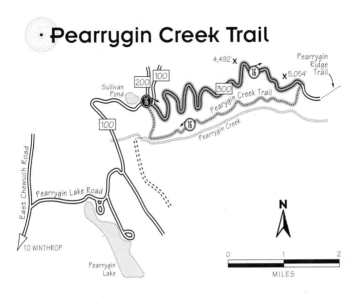

perhaps a bike trail marker. There is no classic trail-head marker. This is the top of Pearrygin Creek Trail. A thin slot entry into the woods will open up within a few yards to become the trail.

9.2 Pass through a barbed-wire gate. Just beyond it a wide cattle trail heads steeply up to the right. Take it. It climbs out of the creek bed, joins a primitive road, and then a trail leading back to Sullivan Pond. It is possible to get lost, but following the most used (by cows?) track on the path of least resistance always seems to work.

10.4 Rejoin FS 100 next to Sullivan Pond.

Pearrygin Ridge Trail

Location: The trail climbs the ridgeline 10 miles northeast of Winthrop, beyond Pearrygin Lake State Park.

Distance: 11 miles out and back.

Time: 3 hours.

Elevation gain: 3,000 feet out and back.

Tread: All singletrack.

Season: Late spring to fall.

Aerobic level: Strenuous.

Technical difficulty: 5.

Hazards: This trail is high in altitude, remote, and little used. Any accident would be very serious. There are many steep, rough, and difficult sections.

Highlights: Interesting, challenging riding for the technically skilled rider. There are great views from Pearrygin Peak. The high altitude (from 4,800 to 6,600 feet) and tree-

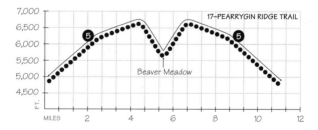

shaded riding make it a good choice for a hot day. Connections with Pearrygin Creek Trail (Ride 16) and Blue Buck Trail make a very long loop possible.

Land status: Okanogan Wenatchee National Forest, Methow Ranger District.

Maps: Green Trails, Doe Mountain, WA–No. 52; Green Trails, Tiffany Mountain, WA–No. 53; USFS Tonasket W1/2 Winthrop E1/2 Ranger District map.

Access: Leave Winthrop heading north on East Chewuch Road. At 1.5 miles take the signed turnoff right to Pearrygin Lake. Continue past the lake; the road turns to gravel and climbs. At the signed junction turn left toward Sullivan Pond on FS 100. Climb about 2 miles; continue past Sullivan Pond and past the nearby left turn to FS 200. Just past that is another signed junction where FS 100 turns left. Continue straight on FS 300 to the road's end and trailhead at 12.3 miles. It is 0.6 miles beyond the Pearrygin Creek Trailhead.

· Pearrygin Ridge Trail

The ride

0.0 The unmarked trail starts from the very end of the road. It climbs through a shady forest of small trees.

1.9 The trail crosses Pearrygin Creek, then climbs steeply up to the ridge.

2.5 Junction with the side trail to Pearrygin Peak. This leads—in 0.4 mile and 410 vertical feet—to the abandoned lookout site on the peak. It's a worthwhile endpoint for an out-and-back trip. The main trail continues along the ridgetop.

3.8 The trail climbs a steep but short cliff band and then climbs the ridge in steps to a high point of 6,589 feet.

4.3 The last high point of the ridge, at 6,415 feet. From here the trail descends the north slope of the ridge. The final 900 vertical feet are steep and twisty.

5.5 Beaver Meadow. You can turn around here for an excellent out-and-back ride. Or continue south along the western edge of Beaver Meadow to reach the Blue Buck Trail, which can be ridden back down to Winthrop. The distance given is for the out-and-back ride.

11.0 Return to trailhead and car.

Tiffany Mountain Loop

Location: 22 miles east of Winthrop.

Distance: 10.4 miles.

Time: 3 hours.

Elevation gain: 2,300 feet; another 600 feet if you hike or bike (very difficult) to the summit.

Tread: 6.7 miles on singletrack; 3.7 miles on gravel road.

Season: Summer and fall.

Aerobic level: Strenuous.

Technical difficulty: 4; 5 if you climb and descend from the summit of Tiffany Mountain.

Hazards: Some trail sections have serious exposure to falls, combined with technical difficulty.

Walk where you feel uncomfortable. The high altitude means there can be extreme and rapid changes in the weather.

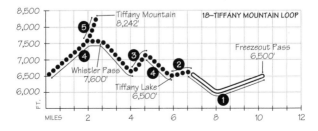

Highlights: Beautiful high-mountain scenery. The altitude keeps the route cool on a hot summer day. A side trip to Tiffany Mountain's summit is even cooler and more beautiful.

Land status: Okanogan Wenatchee National Forest; Methow Ranger District.

Maps: Green Trails, Tiffany Mountain, WA–No. 53; USFS Tonasket W1/2 Winthrop E1/2 Ranger District map.

Access: From the center of Winthrop drive northeast up the hill and turn right onto East Chewuch Road (County Road 9137). Follow that 6.4 miles until you turn right at the junction with Boulder Creek Road (FS 37). Keep right, staying on FS 37 at the junction with First Butte Road (FS 800). Continue to the junction with the Tiffany Lake road (FS 39). Turn left on FS 39 and go all the way to Freezeout Pass, 6,500 feet, at 21.5 miles. Park next to the Freezeout Ridge Trailhead.

The ride

0.0 Start up the Freezeout Ridge Trail. The lower part of the trail is quite difficult, with periodic short rock gardens.

2.0 The trees here have thinned to timberline-level tundra. There is a cairn where the trail turns straight up toward Tiffany Mountain's summit. Look right for another cairn, which marks the way to Whistler Pass and the loop trip. The tread near the junction of the trails is almost invisible—use the cairns to find the path. If possible take the side trip up to the summit. If you like technical riding, take your bike along; if you are not into trials-type downhill, just go for the beautiful hike and the top-of-the-world view.

· Tiffany Mountain Loop

2.7   Whistler Pass. Climb up, north, perhaps 100 yards from the sign marking the pass, to find the trail going northeast over the edge toward Tiffany Lake.

3.2   Junction with trail 373, coming up from Conconully. Take the left branch, toward Tiffany Lake. The trail is rough in places. It drops, then climbs over a pass between Tiffany and Middle Tiffany Mountains, and then drops again to Tiffany Lake.

5.7 Tiffany Lake, 6,500 feet. From here the trail climbs gently to the trailhead.

6.7 Tiffany Lake Trailhead. Turn left onto FS 39. The road drops, then climbs up to Freezeout Pass.

10.4 Freezeout Pass and your car.

Falls Creek—8-Mile Ridge Loop

Location: 22 miles north of Winthrop, near the Chewuch River, and bordering the Pasayten Wilderness.

Distance: 13 miles.

Time: 4 hours.

Elevation gain: 3,500 feet, including a side trip to the summit of Burch Mountain (7,782 feet).

Tread: 13 miles on singletrack.

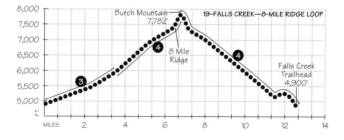

· Falls Creek

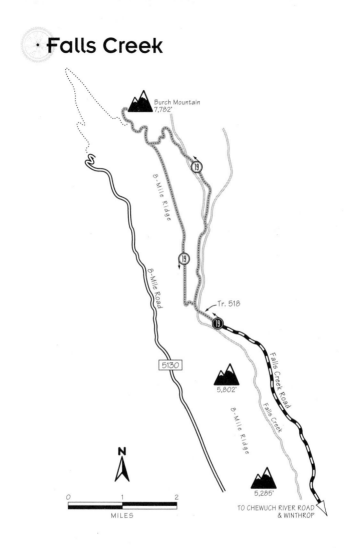

Burch Mountain
7,782'

⑲

⑲

8-Mile Ridge

8-Mile Road

Tr. 518

⑲

5130

5,802'

8-Mile Ridge

Falls Creek Road

Falls Creek

5,285'

N

0   1   2
MILES

TO CHEWUCH RIVER ROAD
& WINTHROP

Season: Summer and fall.

Aerobic level: Strenuous.

Technical difficulty: 4.

Hazards: This is a high-mountain environment with drastic weather changes possible. It's easy to get lost on upper 8-Mile Ridge. There is often winter damage to the trail on the ridge. Ask at a local sport shop about the state of the trail.

Highlights: Ultrascenic ridgetop ride complete with a high summit. Great trail down. High altitude makes it a good choice for a hot summer day.

Land status: Okanogan Wenatchee National Forest, Methow Ranger District.

Maps: Green Trails, Billy Goat Mountain, WA–No. 19; Green Trails, Mazama, WA–No. 51; USFS Winthrop W1/2 Ranger District map.

Access: From Winthrop go north on West Chewuch Road to the junction with Falls Creek Road at 10.6 miles. Turn left and follow the road to the trailhead at its end (21.6 miles).

The ride

- **0.0** Start up the trail. It stays moderate in difficulty for the first 3 miles or so.
- **0.6** Cross Falls Creek. There's a downed tree to help.
- **2.2** Cross the creek again. The trail climbs a little more steeply now.
- **3.6** You'll meet the edge of a swampy area. The trail is flagged and climbs up and around the hanging bog.
- **3.9** Cross Falls Creek yet again.

5.1 Trail junction. This indistinct junction is marked by blue flagging. Turn left onto the more obscure trail. It soon becomes better and climbs away from the creek toward the ridgeline. The other branch goes to the bowl under Burch Mountain.

6.2 Trail junction. The left branch goes to 8-Mile Ridge and returns back to the trailhead. Continue straight to the ridgetop (just 0.1 mile ahead) and then up the ridge to the summit of Burch Mountain (400 vertical feet higher).

6.7 Burch Mountain summit, 7,782 feet. After taking in the view, turn around and head back down to the trail junction.

7.2 Trail junction. The trail from here along the ridge is currently a little obscure. The rule to follow is, don't get far from the right-hand (8-Mile Creek) side of the ridge. It's easy to get pulled to the left, back toward Falls Creek. The trail gets clearer as you go farther.

11.5 The trail turns sharply to the left at the low point in the ridge, in order to return to the trailhead. You must follow it to the left. It's easy to get lost here by continuing forward on a vestigial trail continuing along the ridge.

12.3 Trailhead and end of loop.

Buck Mountain Loop

Location: 8 miles north of Winthrop in the Rendezvous Hills.

Distance: 14 miles.

Time: 2–3 hours.

Elevation gain: 2,200 feet.

Tread: 4.8 miles on singletrack; 2.7 miles on doubletrack; 6.0 miles on gravel.

Season: Spring through fall.

Aerobic level: Moderate.

Technical difficulty: 3.

Hazards: It's easy to get going really fast on parts of this loop. Watch out for the unexpected.

Highlights: Great views of the entire Methow Valley. A combination of single- and doubletrack enjoyable by every rider. This route is one of the most popular in the Methow Valley.

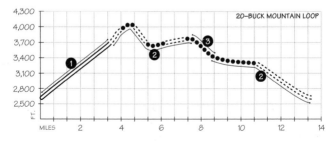

Land status: Okanagan Wenatchee National Forest, Methow Ranger District.

Maps: Green Trails, Doe Mountain, WA–No. 52; USFS Winthrop W1/2 Ranger District map.

Access: Head north from Winthrop on West Chewuch Road 6.1 miles to the turnoff for Cub Creek. Turn left, go 2 miles further, and park just where the pavement ends (First Creek Ranch).

The ride

0.0 Start up Cub Creek Road. Keep right to stay on FS 100. Don't get pulled left on FS 52 to either Rendezvous Pass or Mazama. After 1,100 feet of climbing on the road, you will reach the DEER COUNTRY sign and the turnoff to the Buck Mountain Loop.

3.4 The road branches. Climb to the right up doubletrack, which is marked with a yellow bike route marker. These markers are posted at every ambiguous junction.

3.7 Junction. The doubletrack splits; turn right. The doubletrack becomes singletrack as it climbs.

4.4 The trail reaches a high point. It turns back into doubletrack as it swoops down.

5.2 Keep left where the trail breaks off from the doubletrack. The junction is marked with a yellow marker on a tree below.

5.3 Another junction. Turn left onto singletrack, breaking through the brush.

7.7 A high point following a short, steep climb. The trail then plunges down a short section that used to be steep and ugly but now has a moderate zigzag descent.

· Buck Mountain Loop

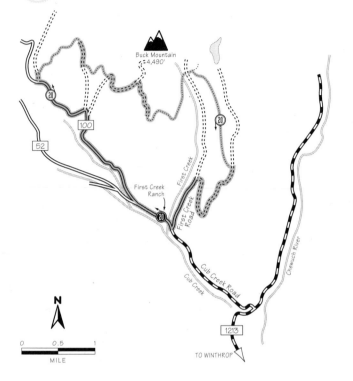

10.7 An exhilarating singletrack downhill leads to First Creek Road, which then takes you even faster back to Cub Creek Road.

13.4 Junction with Cub Creek Road. Turn right and ride up to the parking area.

13.5 End of loop.

Cougar Lake Loop

Location: 4 miles southeast of Winthrop near Davis Lake.

Distance: 7 miles.

Time: 1 hour.

Elevation gain: 1,000 feet.

Tread: 5 miles on gravel road; 2 miles on doubletrack.

Season: Spring through fall.

Aerobic level: Moderate.

Technical Difficulty: 1.

Hazards: Watch out for vehicles.

Highlights: Scenic views of the Sawtooth Wilderness and Pipestone Canyon. An easy ride, fun for everyone.

Land status: Washington State Fish and Wildlife Department.

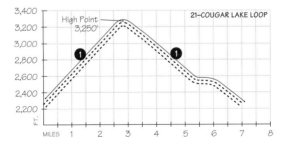

Maps: Green Trails, Twisp, WA–No. 84; USFS Tonasket W1/2 Winthrop E1/2 Ranger District map.

Option: This route can also be used to access the two Pipestone Canyon loops described in this guide (Rides 10, 11). This option would be preferable if you were biking from Winthrop, rather than driving to the trailheads.

Access: From Winthrop center (the four-way stop), head south out of town on Washington 20. At the bridge over the Methow River, go straight instead of turning right to cross the bridge. Dogleg 1 block further east (away from the river, following the arterial signs) and continue out of town on Twisp-Winthrop Road. At 2.2 miles turn left at the intersection with Bear Creek Road. Continue past the Davis Lake turnoff and park just where the asphalt ends at the intersection with Campbell Lake Road (4.0 miles).

The ride

0.0 Start pedaling up the road toward Campbell Lake.

0.6 Switchback. Views appear of Oval and Hoodoo Peaks.

1.2 Junction with turnoff left to Cougar Lake. Take it. The road becomes a good doubletrack.

1.5 Another junction. Keep climbing straight. Turning right would lead back to Campbell Lake. That would be a good way to connect with the Pipestone loops.

2.1 The road levels off. Good views back to Pipestone Canyon.

2.8 The true high point of the route. Just ahead is the turnoff to Cougar Lake.

2.9 Cougar Lake junction. Cougar Lake is to the right. The route continues straight ahead.

• Cougar Lake Loop

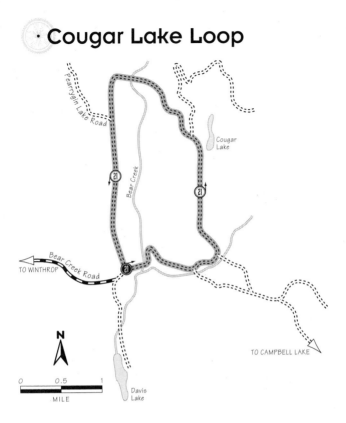

3.2 Bear Creek junction. Keep left. The road becomes improved gravel again. It drops steadily to the next junction.

5.2 Junction with Pearrygin Lake Road. Keep left. Climb a small hill and pass the game department station.

7.0 End of loop.

Sun Mountain Area

Sun Mountain has an excellent trail system and is very popular, with many trails of easy to moderate difficulty.

Sun Mountain Easy Loop

Location: 8 miles west of Winthrop.

Distance: 6.1 miles.

Time: 1 hour.

Elevation gain: 400 feet.

Tread: All doubletrack.

Season: Spring through fall.

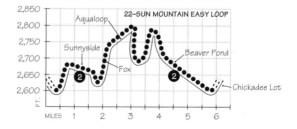

82

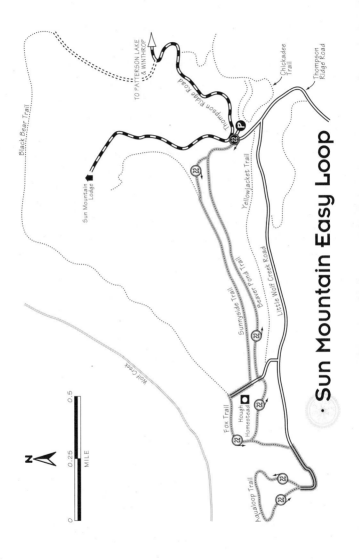

· Sun Mountain Easy Loop

N

0   0.25   0.5
MILE

Wolf Creek

Aqualoop Trail

Fox Trail

Hough Homestead

Sunnyside Trail

Beaver Pond Trail

Little Wolf Creek Road

Yellowjacket Trail

Sun Mountain Lodge

Black Bear Trail

Thompson Ridge Road

TO PATTERSON LAKE & WINTHROP

Chickadee Trail

Thompson Ridge Road

Aerobic level: Easy.

Technical difficulty: 2.

Hazards: Not many. Don't get lost and circle endlessly.

Highlights: Good views of Wolf Creek and Mount Gardner. An easy trail that's still fun for most riders. It is well signed, so the many trail junctions shouldn't be too confusing.

Land status: Private and Okanogan Wenatchee National Forest, Methow Ranger District.

Maps: Get the Sun Mountain Recreational map from a local sport shop.

Access: From Winthrop drive south out of town, over the Methow River Bridge. Instead of turning to the left with the highway, continue straight, following signs for Sun Mountain Lodge. At 8 miles you'll reach the junction with Thompson Ridge Road. Turn left onto that and then almost immediately left again into the Chickadee parking lot.

The ride

0.0 Leave the Chickadee parking lot via its lower entrance, ride a few yards down the road, then turn left to enter the trail system. You will see the Beaver Pond Bridge ahead.

0.1 Cross the bridge onto Beaver Pond Trail.

0.4 Turn right onto Short Cut Trail, heading uphill.

0.7 Junction with Sunnyside Trail; turn left.

1.6 Reach the Hough Homestead Shelter. Turn right onto Lower Fox Trail.

1.8 Junction with Black Bear Trail. Keep left, staying on Fox Trail.

2.1 Junction with Upper Fox Trail and spur to Aqualoop Trail. Keep right on the way to Aqualoop.

2.2	Another junction. Again keep right. Follow signs for Aqualoop.
4.1	Junction with spur to Fox Trail; turn left.
4.2	Another trail junction; turn left.
4.3	Junction with Upper Fox Trail; turn right.
4.5	Four-way junction. Turn left over the bridge, then right.
4.6	Enter Beaver Pond Trail.
6.0	Thompson Ridge Road. Turn right, then almost immediately left into the Chickadee parking lot.
6.1	End of the loop.

Sun Mountain Fun Route

Location: 8 miles west of Winthrop.

Distance: 7.3 miles.

Time: 1–2 hours.

Elevation gain: 790 feet.

Tread: 6.6 miles on singletrack; 0.7 mile on doubletrack.

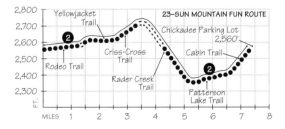

Season: Spring through fall.

Aerobic level: Moderate.

Technical difficulty: 2.

Hazards: There is some exposed hillside on the trail along Patterson Lake.

Highlights: This is an easy loop on rolling, twisting, fast trails—pure fun to ride.

Land status: Private and Okanogan Wenatchee National Forest, Methow Ranger District.

Maps: Get the Sun Mountain Recreational map from a local sport shop.

Access: From Winthrop drive south out of town, over the Methow River Bridge. Instead of turning to the left with the highway, continue straight, following signs for Sun Mountain Lodge. At 8 miles you'll reach the junction with Thompson Ridge Road. Turn left there and then almost immediately left again into the Chickadee parking lot.

The ride

0.0 Leave the Chickadee parking lot at its lower end and descend on Thompson Ridge Road.

0.1 Turn left and enter Rodeo Trail.

1.4 Rodeo ends at a four-way intersection. Turn left and climb up to the entrance of Yellowjacket Trail.

1.5 Turn left onto Yellowjacket Trail.

2.5 Trail junction; keep straight.

2.6 Another junction; keep right.

2.6 Junction with Little Wolf Creek Road. Cross it and enter Criss-Cross Trail.

3.4 Junction with Thompson Ridge Road. Cross it and continue on the spur on the other side.

· Sun Mountain Fun Route

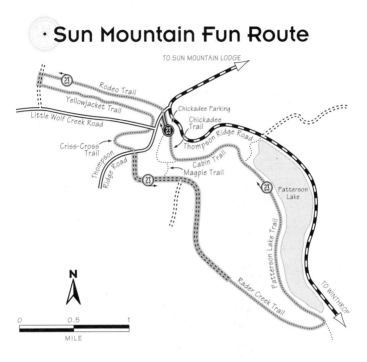

3.5 Entrance to Magpie Trail; pass it.

3.6 T-junction. Go left onto Rader Creek Trail. This descends rapidly, turning from double- to singletrack lower down.

5.2 Rader Creek Trail ends. Turn left onto Patterson Lake Trail. This beautiful singletrack follows the western shore of the lake.

6.7 Junction with Cabin Trail; turn left.

7.1 Junction with Chickadee Trail. Either way takes you to the parking lot.

7.3 Chickadee parking lot.

Sun Mountain Scenic Ride

Location: 8 miles west of Winthrop in the Sun Mountain Lodge trail system.

Distance: 11.1 miles.

Time: 1½–2½ hours.

Elevation gain: 1,400 feet.

Tread: 2.7 miles on singletrack; 5.2 miles on doubletrack; 3.2 miles on gravel road.

Season: Spring through fall.

Aerobic level: Moderate.

Technical difficulty: 2.

Hazards: Some of the Patterson Lake Trail has steep side-hill exposure. Be careful not to go too fast on lower Rader

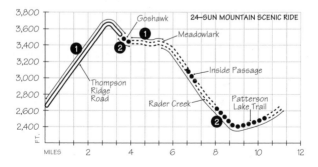

Creek Trail, where there are small rock gardens amid faster trail.

Highlights: Views, views, views. Beyond that, like most Sun Mountain routes, it's a moderate ride that's fun for every rider.

Land status: Part private and part Okanogan Wenatchee National Forest, Methow Ranger District.

Maps: Get the Sun Mountain Recreational map from a local sport shop.

Access: From Winthrop drive south out of town, over the Methow River Bridge. Instead of turning to the left with the highway, continue straight, following signs for Sun Mountain Lodge. At 8 miles you'll reach the junction with Thompson Ridge Road. Turn left onto that and then almost immediately left again into the Chickadee parking lot.

The ride

0.0 From the parking lot, start riding south, up Thompson Ridge Road.

3.0 The top of the climb, just past the top of Upper Inside Passage trail.

3.4 Turn left onto Goshawk, a short but sweet single-track. This is easy to miss, since there is no prominent sign.

3.8 Junction with Meadowlark; turn left. This double-track cruises around the side of the mountain. Far-reaching views abound.

4.6 Junction with Blue Jay. Keep going straight on Meadowlark.

6.6 Junction with Upper Inside Passage; keep right.

6.7 Junction with Lower Inside Passage. Turn right and go downhill.

· Sun Mountain Scenic Ride

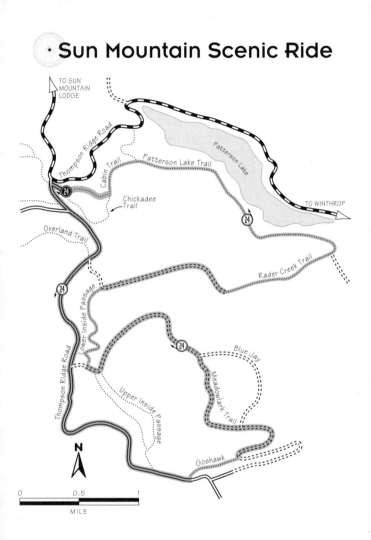

TO SUN
MOUNTAIN
LODGE

Thompson Ridge Road

Cabin Trail

Patterson Lake Trail

Patterson Lake

Chickadee
Trail

TO WINTHROP

Overland Trail

Rader Creek Trail

Lower Inside Passage

Thompson Ridge Road

Upper Inside Passage

Blue Jay

Meadowlark Trail

Goshawk

N

0   0.5   1
MILE

7.4	Junction with Rader Creek Trail. Turn right onto this fast and fun downhill.
8.9	Turn left onto Patterson Lake Trail. This is a beautiful singletrack rolling around the shore of the lake.
10.4	Junction. Turn left onto Cabin Trail.
10.9	Junction with Chickadee Trail. Either way takes you to the parking lot. Right is a little shorter.
11.1	Back to the parking lot and end of the loop.

Sun Mountain Top to Bottom

Location: 2.4 miles west of Winthrop.

Distance: 15.6 miles.

Time: 3 hours.

Elevation gain: 2,300 feet.

Tread: 6.2 miles on singletrack; 5.7 miles on doubletrack; 3.7 miles on gravel road.

Season: Spring through fall.

Aerobic level: Moderate.

Technical difficulty: 3.

Hazards: Trees almost touch the trail on parts of Pete's Dragon, just where you will be speeding downhill. You will also go fast down the Winthrop Trail. Watch out for other trail users.

Highlights: A long climb is followed by a long and wonderfully varied downhill. Great views of the Methow Valley from Black Bear Trail.

Land status: Okanogan Wenatchee National Forest, Methow Ranger District.

Maps: Green Trails, Twisp, WA–No. 84; Green Trails, Buttermilk Butte, WA–No. 83.

Access: From Winthrop drive south, over the Methow River Bridge. Instead of turning to the left with the highway, continue straight, following signs for Sun Mountain Lodge. At 2.4 miles there is a hidden entrance to a parking space on the right. This is signed WINTHROP TRAIL. Park there.

The ride

- **0.0** Follow the trail around the gate and onto the dirt road beyond.
- **0.4** Junction.; turn right. The main road is gated closed for private use, so the route makes a detour around a short section of it, using another primitive road.
- **0.8** Rejoin the main road. Turn right.
- **1.9** Junction. Keep left, up the hill, on the well-used trail.
- **2.8** Cross the paved road. Pick up the trail on the other side.

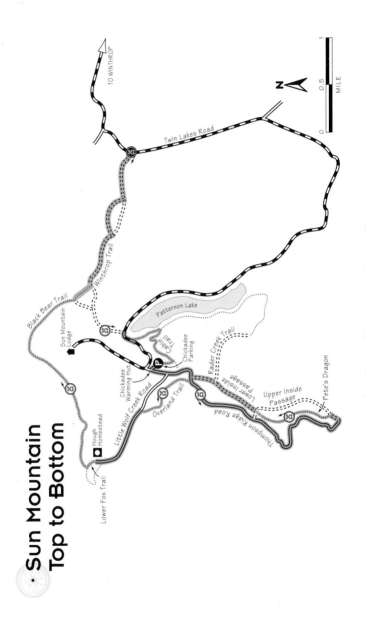

Sun Mountain
Top to Bottom

TO WINTHROP

Twin Lakes Road

N

MILE
0   0.5   1

Black Bear Trail

Winthrop Trail

Sun Mountain Lodge

Patterson Lake

Cabin Trail

Chickadee Warming Hut

Little Wolf Creek Road

Chickadee Parking

Rader Creek Trail

Hough Homestead

Overland Trail

Thompson Ridge Road

Lower Fox Trail

Lower Inside Passage

Upper Inside Passage

Pete's Dragon

3.0	Cross the entrance road to Patterson Lake Cabins. Pick up Cabin Trail on the other side.
3.2	Go straight, staying on Cabin Trail.
3.6	Junction with Chickadee Trail. Turn right, pass the Chickadee Warming Hut, then go out the northwest exit to Thompson Ridge Road.
3.8	Start climbing up Thompson Ridge Road.
6.8	The end of the climb. Turn left down Upper Inside Passage.
6.9	Turn left onto Pete's Dragon. The sign might be hard to see, but a large boulder marks the junction. The trail is a narrow forest-lined singletrack downhill.
7.8	The end of Pete's Dragon. Turn left to find the top of Lower Inside Passage.
7.9	Turn right onto Lower Inside Passage.
8.5	Junction with Rader Creek Trail. Stay left and traverse back to Thompson Ridge Road.
8.8	Cross Thompson Ridge Road and enter Overland Trail on the other side.
9.7	Junction with Little Wolf Creek Road; turn left.
10.4	Turn right and go down Homestead Trail. Go past the shelter.
10.6	Enter Lower Fox Trail.
10.8	Junction. Turn right onto Black Bear. This starts as doubletrack but soon becomes beautiful singletrack, mostly descending.
12.3	There is a steep climb. Most attempts to ride it fail, but it can be done (best when the ground is damp).
13.5	Black Bear empties onto doubletrack. Just above this is another junction; turn left. This spur takes you back to Winthrop Trail.
13.7	Junction with Winthrop Trail. Go left.
15.6	A fast downhill ride takes you back to your car.

Elbow Coulee Loop

Location: 5.5 miles west of Twisp.

Distance: 9.8 miles. With the optional side trips the distance is 15.8 miles.

Time: 1½ hours. With the optional side trips the time is an additional 1 to 2 hours.

Elevation gain: 1,030 feet; 2,060 feet with the side trips.

Tread: 2.3 miles on doubletrack; 4.8 miles on gravel; 2.7 miles on pavement.

Season: Spring through fall.

Aerobic level: Moderate. There is only one steep climb (just 200 vertical feet).

Technical difficulty: 2.

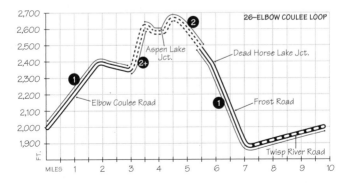

·Elbow Coulee Loop

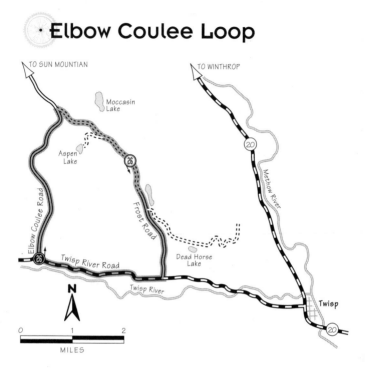

Hazards: You might encounter a gravel truck on Elbow Coulee Road.

Highlights: This is an easy ride, close to Twisp, which melts out early, stays ridable late into fall, and is especially scenic in the spring, when flowers cover the hillsides.

Options: This ride is easily extended by doing side trips to Aspen Lake and/or Dead Horse Lake.

Land status: Washington State Department of Fish and Wildlife.

Maps: Green Trails, Twisp, WA–No. 84; USFS Twisp Ranger District map.

Access: From Twisp drive west up Twisp River Road 5.5 miles to the turnoff for Elbow Coulee Road. Park there.

The ride

0.0   Ride up Elbow Coulee Road.

3.0   Junction. Turn right and go up the steep doubletrack.

3.8   Gate. Climb over the chained cattle gate and continue on the doubletrack.

4.1   Aspen Lake Junction. To do the loop continue straight. Turn right to get to Aspen Lake. The side trip (0.6 miles and 400 vertical feet) is well worth it.

4.4   Gate. Go through it and close it behind you.

5.5   Pass through another gate; you are now on the much-improved Frost Road.

5.8   Junction with doubletrack to Dead Horse Lake and beyond. Another worthy side trip. You can ride until you are on a hillside overlooking Twisp. Stop at the gateless fence crossing the trail; private property lies beyond. The out-and-back trip is 5.4 miles and 630 vertical feet. To complete the loop continue south on Frost Road.

7.1   Junction with Twisp River Road. Turn right and pedal up the pavement.

9.8   Elbow Coulee Road and car. End of the loop.

Twisp and Loup Loup Areas

The Loup Loup area has many bikeable dirt roads. We've included just one ride but it's a good example of what can be created. Twisp River has just two legal trail rides but they are both notably long and interesting.

27

Finley Canyon Loop

Location: 8 miles southeast of Twisp in the hills south of Loup Loup Pass.

Distance: 19.5 miles.

Time: 3–5 hours.

Elevation gain: 2,600 feet.

Tread: 0.2 miles on singletrack; 15.4 miles on dirt road; 3.9 miles on paved road.

Season: Spring through fall.

Aerobic level: Moderate.

Technical difficulty: 2.

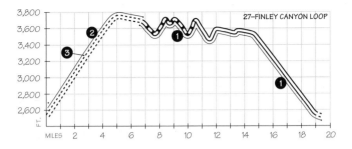

Hazards: You may meet vehicles on the paved section. In hunting season vehicles could be anywhere.

Highlights: A long, desolate, dirt-road ride around Finley Canyon.

Land status: Okanogan National Forest, Methow Ranger District.

Maps: Green Trails, Twisp, WA–No. 84; Green Trails, Loup Loup, WA–No. 85; USFS Twisp Ranger District map.

Access: From Twisp go south 2 miles on Washington 20. Follow it when it turns left toward Loup Loup Pass. At 3.8 miles take a right turn onto Lower Beaver Creek Road. Ride 0.2 mile farther and take a left onto Finley Canyon Road. At 7.7 miles park in the opening just past the cattle guard.

The ride

0.0   Start riding east on the road up the canyon.

0.4   Turn left onto the spur and ride around the pond in the middle of the canyon. If the pond is dry, keep riding straight ahead.

·Finley Canyon Loop

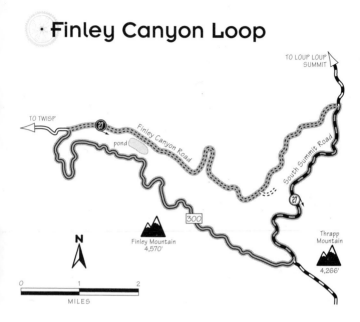

0.8 Rejoin Finley Canyon Road. It gradually climbs on the left-hand (north) side of the canyon.

2.5 The road narrows to singletrack and crosses a gully.

2.7 The road resumes.

3.9 The road forks; stay left.

5.3 A series of road-closure bumps and a cattle stock trough. Keep going.

6.7 Junction with the paved South Summit Road (FS 41); Turn right.

10.6 Junction with FS 300; turn right.

19.0 Junction with Finley Canyon Road. Turn right and pedal back to your car.

19.5 End of loop.

28

Twisp River Trail

Location: 12 miles west of Twisp.

Distance: 29-mile loop. There are many shorter and easier variants.

Time: 4–5 hours. Shorter loops are popular.

Elevation gain: 2,250 feet.

Tread: 15.1 miles on singletrack; 3.8 miles on pavement; 10.1 miles on gravel road.

Season: Late spring through fall.

Aerobic level: Moderate.

Technical difficulty: 4 on the 2.5 miles above South Creek Trail; 3 thereafter.

Hazards: The top section of the trail is steep and rocky. There is a short scree slope crossing (only 0.2 mile long) midway.

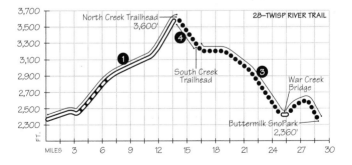

Highlights: Scenic in the upper sections. It's easy to select shorter and easier loops lower on the trail. It melts out relatively early due to the low elevation.

Land status: Okanogan Wenatchee National Forest, Methow District.

Maps: Green Trails, Buttermilk Butte, WA–No. 83; Green Trails, Stehekin, WA–No. 82; USFS Twisp Ranger District map.

Access: From the center of Twisp, follow Twisp River Road 10.9 miles to the Buttermilk Creek turnoff. Cross the bridge and turn right at the fork. At 12.4 miles reach the Buttermilk SnoPark and park there.

The ride

0.0   From Buttermilk SnoPark start pedaling up the road (FS 4420, the south side Twisp River Road).
2.9   Cross the bridge over War Creek.
3.3   Turn right and cross the bridge over the Twisp River.
3.4   Go left and continue up the main Twisp River Road (FS 44).
6.4   Pass the Slate Lake Trailhead.
7.2   Junction with Mystery Camp Road. Pavement ends. Continue straight.
10.8 Scatter Creek Trailhead.
11.3 South Creek Trailhead and campground.
13.9 Turn right and pedal up to the North Creek Trailhead. Find the Twisp River Trailhead at the far end of the parking lot.
14.0 The trail drops and crosses the road. The segment from here to the junction with South Creek Trail (2.4 miles) is technically much more difficult than the rest of the trail.

· Twisp River Trail

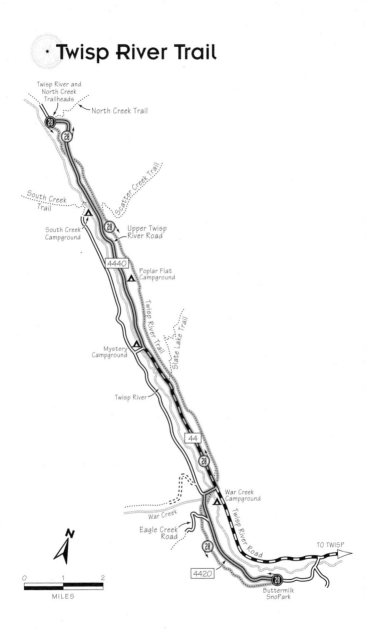

Twisp River and
North Creek
Trailheads

North Creek Trail

Scatter Creek Trail

South Creek
Trail

South Creek
Campground

Upper Twisp
River Road

4440

Poplar Flat
Campground

Twisp River Trail

Mystery
Campground

Slate Lake Trail

Twisp River

44

War Creek
Campground

War Creek

Eagle Creek
Road

Twisp River Road

TO TWISP

4420

Buttermilk
SnoPark

N

0   1   2
MILES

15.1 The trail crosses the road again.

16.5 Junction with spur to South Creek trailhead. Continue straight.

17.1 Junction with the Scatter Creek Trail. Continue on Twisp River Trail.

19.1 Junction with the spur to Poplar Flat Campground. Continue straight.

19.7 Start of 0.2-mile-long section of scree slopes (not difficult).

21.7 Junction with Slate Lake Trail. Continue straight.

25.0 The trail crosses the road at War Creek Bridge.

25.5 The trail crosses the south side of Twisp River Road (FS 4420) and resumes on the other side.

26.2 The trail crosses Eagle Creek Road.

28.3 The high point on this segment of trail.

29.0 Buttermilk SnoPark.

Canyon Creek Ridge

Location: 13 miles west of Twisp.

Distance: 12.2 miles.

Time: 6 hours.

Elevation gain: 4,000 feet.

Tread: All singletrack (at best).

Season: Summer and fall.

Aerobic level: Strenuous.

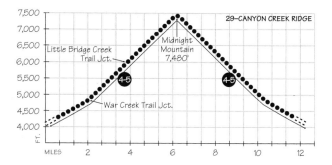

Technical difficulty: 5.

Hazards: This is a high-altitude ride with exposure to sudden, severe weather changes. The trail is often rough and technically difficult. In places it is obscure.

Highlights: The stellar views and the isolation, the difficulty, the length, and the altitude of the trail.

Land status: Okanogan Wenatchee National Forest, Methow Ranger District.

Maps: Green Trails, Buttermilk Butte, WA–No. 83; USFS Twisp Ranger District map.

Access: From Twisp, drive up Twisp River Road 11.4 miles, then turn right onto FS 100. Follow this past the junction with FS 110 and around the nose of the north branch of Canyon Creek Ridge. Shortly after a right-hand turn, where there is a cattle trough at 16.3 miles, an unnumbered spur road takes off to the left. It may have a cairn. Park there.

• Canyon Creek Ridge

The ride

0.0 Ride up the spur until you get to a saddle on the ridge.

0.4 From the saddle ride up the ridge, looking for the path of least resistance. There will be a rudimentary trail.

1.9 The trail becomes well defined.

2.0 The trail meets the old (very steep and rough) trail coming up from War Creek Campground. Continue following the ridge.

3.8 The trail meets another trail coming up from Little Bridge Creek. This is another possible way to access the ridge. Its location is not shown correctly on the maps. Its unmarked trailhead is near the top of FS 4415-100, a spur of Little Bridge Creek Road (FS 4415).

4.6 The trail turns right to traverse under 3 A.M. Mountain.

6.1 Midnight Mountain summit, 7,480 feet. From here turn around and ride back down.

12.2 Back to your car.

A Short Index of Rides

Glossary

ATB: All-terrain bicycle; a.k.a. mountain bike, sprocket rocket, fat tire flyer.

ATV: All-terrain vehicle; in this book ATV refers to motorbikes and three- and four-wheelers designed for off-road use.

Bail: To get off the bike, usually in a hurry, whether or not you mean to. Often a last resort.

Bunny hop: Leaping up, while riding, and lifting both wheels off the ground to jump over an obstacle (or for sheer joy).

Clamper cramps: That burning, cramping sensation experienced in the hands during extended breaking.

Clean: To ride without touching a foot (or other body part) to the ground; to ride a tough section successfully.

Clipless: A type of pedal with a binding that accepts a special cleat on the soles of bike shoes. The cleat clicks in for more control and efficient pedaling, and out for safe landings (in theory).

Contour: A line on a topographic map showing a continuous elevation level over uneven ground. Also used as a verb to indicate a fairly easy or moderate grade: "The trail contours around the west flank of the mountain before the final grunt to the top."

Dab: To put a foot or hand down (or hold on to or lean on a tree or other support) while riding. If you have to dab, then you haven't ridden that piece of trail **clean**.

Downfall: Trees that have fallen across the trail.

Doubletrack: A trail, jeep road, ATV route, or other track with two distinct ribbons of **tread,** typically with grass growing in between. No matter which side you choose, the other rut always looks smoother.

Endo: Lifting the rear wheel off the ground and riding (or abruptly not riding) on the front wheel only. Also known, at various degrees of control and finality, as a "nose wheelie," "going over the handlebars," and a "face plant."

Fall line: The angle and direction of a slope; the **line** you follow when gravity is in control and you aren't.

Graded: When a gravel road is scraped level to smooth out the washboards and potholes, it has been graded. In this book, a road is listed as graded only if it is regularly maintained. Not all such roads are graded every year, however.

Granny gear: The innermost and smallest of the three chainrings on the bottom bracket spindle (where the pedals and crank arms attach to the bike's frame). Shift down to your granny gear (and up to the biggest cog on the rear hub) to find your lowest (easiest) gear for climbing.

Hammer: To ride hard; derived from how it feels afterward: "I'm hammered."

Hammerhead: Someone who actually enjoys feeling **hammered.** A Type-A rider who goes hard and fast all the time.

Kelly hump: An abrupt mound of dirt across the road or trail. These are common on old logging roads and skidder tracks; they are placed there to block vehicle access. At high speeds, they become launching pads for bikes and inadvertent astronauts.

Line: The route (or trajectory) between or over obstacles or through turns. **Tread** or trail refers to the ground you're riding on; the line is the path you choose within the tread (and exists mostly in the eye of the beholder).

Off-the-seat: Moving your butt behind the bike seat and over the rear tire; used for control on extremely steep descents. This position increases braking power, helps prevent endos, and reduces skidding.

Portage: To carry the bike, usually up a steep hill, across unridable obstacles, or through a stream.

Quads: Thigh muscles (short for quadriceps); or maps in the USGS topographic series (short for quadrangles). Nice quads of either kind can help get you out of trouble in the backcountry.

Ratcheting: Also known as backpedaling; pedaling backward to avoid hitting rocks or other obstacles with your pedals.

Sidehill: A place where the trail crosses a slope. If the **tread** is narrow, keep your inside (uphill) pedal up to avoid hitting the ground. If the tread tilts downhill, you may have to use some body language to keep the bike plumb or vertical to avoid slipping out.

Singletrack: A trail, game run, or other track with only one ribbon of **tread.** But this is like defining an orgasm as a muscle cramp. Good singletrack is pure fun.

Spur: A side road or trail that splits off from the main route.

Surf: Riding through loose gravel or sand, when the wheels sway from side to side. Also heavy surf: frequent and difficult obstacles.

Suspension: A bike with front suspension has a shock-absorbing fork or stem. Rear suspension absorbs shock between the rear wheel and frame. A bike with both is said to be *fully suspended.*

Switchbacks: A zigzag, or a steep slope, across the **fall line** to ease the gradient of the climb. Well-designed switchbacks make a turn with at least an eight-foot radius and remain fairly level within the turn itself. These are rare, however, and cyclists often struggle to ride through sharply angled, sloping switchbacks.

Track stand: Balancing on a bike in one place, without rolling forward appreciably. To execute a track stand, cock the front wheel to one side and bring that pedal up to the one or two o'clock position. Now control your side-to-side balance by applying pressure on the pedals and brakes and changing the angle of the front wheel, as needed. It takes practice but really comes in handy at stoplights, on **switchbacks,** and when trying to free a foot before falling.

Tread: The riding surface, particularly regarding singletrack.

Water bar: A log, rock, or other barrier placed in the **tread** to divert water off the trail and prevent erosion. Peeled logs can be slippery and cause bad falls, especially when they angle sharply across the trail.

Whoop-dee-doo: A series of **kelly humps** used to keep vehicles off trails. Watch your speed or do the dreaded top-tube tango.

About the Author

Steve Barnett has lived in the Methow Valley since 1979 and has been mountain biking since the invention of the sport. Among his other published works are two books about ski touring.

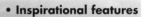